NEVER LOOK BACK

NEVER LOOK BACK

The Owen Lowery Story

V. G. HARLEY

HIGHLAND BOOKS

ISBN 0 946616 72 8

Sketches: *Cathy Walker*

Cover design: *Diane Drummond*

Typeset by Rowland Phototypesetting Limited
Bury St Edmunds, Suffolk
Printed in Great Britain for
HIGHLANDS BOOKS
Broadway House, The Broadway,
Crowborough, East Sussex, TN6 1HQ
by Richard Clay Limited, Bungay, Suffolk

To Sybil

Chapter 1

On his way to Crystal Palace he didn't let himself think about the events of the next few hours. It was important to steer his mind away from the competition, from his opponents, the mat, the attacks, the holds. He found it best to let his mind float, to look out of the windows and watch the scenery slip away on either side. Perfectly relaxed, he listened lazily to his parents and brother talk about the weekend grocery shopping and neighbourhood news. He began to daydream about the summer.

Inside the grounds his mind snapped to attention, and he strode eagerly towards the familiar doors. He knew Crystal Palace well, since those early years in the sport when he had first entered competitions. The vast complex could not intimidate him. He was in control and already mentally stretching his muscles, limbering up, sensing the blood flow.

In the changing rooms he nodded to friends and exchanged a few words, but preferred to be quiet, letting others clown and shout. 'Strong competition today,' he said to himself, taking nothing for granted. No time to think of past successes. Every match was a new day. This would be the most important in terms of future progress: the winner would be no. 1 in the Young Men's National Squad for the coming year and could go on to qualify for Internationals.

As he always did, Owen moved into gear during the hour before his match. Once into the hall (the *dojo*) he worked up gradually with limbering-up exercises and at the same time caught glimpses of those he was 'pooled' against, and how they handled themselves. He didn't sell anyone short, even those he had beaten in the past. Any one of them could surprise him if he was stupid enough to be complacent.

And he was right: the competition was hard. Even the first matches demanded a lot. And when he reached the semi-finals there was Philip Sullivan from Wigan again, an old adversary. Owen managed to knock him down with a shoulder throw, but it wasn't an easy match. Owen went into the final against Ian Burke of Southampton knowing it would be a close fight, and it was. They went the distance and awaited the judges' decision.

'*Hantei*,' the referee called out to the corner judges. Simultaneously the one on the right held up his white flag voting for Owen and the judge opposite lifted his red flag in favour of Burke. It was up to the referee now. His arm rose towards Owen.

Sybil Lowery uncharacteristically leaped to her feet and cheered her son, but then, seeing Burke's father nearby, sat down grinning. Owen recalled one of last year's triumphs when he was so elated he waved his arms in delight. 'Not done in this sport,' he was told sternly. Now, despite the applause, he contained his joy.

Adam and Owen in their Reading garden

'It wasn't a bad fight,' his coach Don Werner commented, never generous with compliments. But he was smiling. Owen took it as praise.

Eighteen-year-old Owen couldn't be blamed for the elation and confidence surging through him as the family drove back to Reading. What an incredible year it had been! Twelve months earlier, in Bracknell, he'd won the National Youth Tournament, unexpectedly capturing the title from the no. 1 on the Young Men's National Judo Squad. By the summer, he had clocked up more wins, including the British Men's Closed. In Birmingham it was tough-going at the British Schoolboys' Association Trials. There had been lots of good lads of his age in the Midlands, and he recalled what hard work it had been beating a few of them. By the time he'd reached the Under-18 National Championships at Crystal Palace, he'd been quietly confident. Having already won the British Men's title he didn't think he could lose this one, and he didn't.

Such reminiscences, however, couldn't sustain him for long and before Dave pulled into their drive on Falstaff Avenue, Owen was already eager to try something more relaxing with his mates. Some of Mole's homemade brew, perhaps, at whoever's house was conveniently vacated by parents tonight, or, barring that, a few games in the Lowery garage 'poolroom'. He mustn't be up too late, of course. Tomorrow morning meant back to training again, as well as the usual post-mortems at the Club, with Coach Don dissecting the moves of the day before.

Owen had a particular way of sealing off the various parts of his life into airtight 'boxes'. His judo fitted nicely into one of these units and when he was training or competing he gave the sport his serious and undivided attention. Whatever was going on in the outside world – an 'A' level exam, a big date, or World War Three – *nothing* was permitted to break his concentration.

His social life was kept quite separate, and his closest friends were usually schoolmates or those involved in sport other than judo. After the rigours of training or the stress of a match or competition there was nothing so relaxing as a night out with mates, a non-stop flow of beer, practical jokes and ribaldry, staggering home well past midnight or weaving precariously through the streets on his rickety old 'grandpa' cycle with the sit-up-and-beg handlebars.

There was another box marked 'school' which was quite a world away from either judo or the crazy mischief he got up to with his mates. He wasn't a swot, of course, but he could get carried away in classroom debates and he took his English classes more seriously than many others did. He was proud of his voluminous vocabulary, but was amazed when one critic said it was 'squeezed into Miltonesque poems like a stout lady in a pair of jeans'. It was even implied, to his horror, that he should edit or condense his treasured verses! 'That would be like cutting off the Mona Lisa's nose,' he replied indignantly.

Cathy Walker, pretty and brown-haired, was Owen's equal in joking and making up pranks. From the very first it was a wacky sort of friendship. They called each other names and loved to argue about English Literature, their favourite subject. The fact that they often disagreed enhanced the friendship; they both enjoyed a bit of a fight.

Cathy first noticed Owen at a sponsored walk. He was eleven. That summer day of 81 was swelteringly hot and of those who managed to complete the course most walked wearily to the finish. But Owen was way ahead having kept a steady pace. He didn't walk, he ran.

Cathy and Owen had courses in common every year or two, but in the Sixth Form their timetables coincided with 'A' level English four times a week. They were also in the same tutor group.

Sometimes Owen's mischievous humour got him into trouble. When an unsuspecting teacher called upon him to read a poem by Herbert he started out well enough. Then he read:

> Oh that I were an orange-tree, that busy plant!
> Then should I ever laden be, and never want
> Some fruit for Him that dressed me . . .

The absurdity of the picture made Owen guffaw. An orange tree for God? Whatever next? When the furore died down, Cathy was asked to explain it. It wasn't so far-fetched to her, she said; it was a rather fanciful way of saying we can all make an offering to God.

Afterwards Owen tackled her. 'Come on, porker,' he laughed. 'Surely you don't believe all that rubbish?'

There followed an animated exchange of views as they walked from the classroom to the gym. 'Look what religion's done to the people of Northern Ireland,' he reminded her.

'And how do you know they're really Christians?' she asked.

'You *would* say that!' he scoffed.

'Do you think for a moment that anyone who blows up a building full of people is thinking about Christ?' she pressed him.

'All through history people have fought in the name of religion,' he began.

'Oh, I was just waiting for the Crusades! I was wondering when you'd bring that up!'

And the more they argued the more they enjoyed it.

Cathy realised there were other sides to him, too. In one class they were arranging a schedule of work, but Owen said, 'Sorry, I can't be here next week.'

'Why not?' she asked.

'I'm fighting in Malta,' he answered matter-of-factly.

She had heard something about his interest in judo, but never realised that he travelled so far to play. She didn't know that he had a roomful of trophies in his bedroom and that he was already becoming known in clubs throughout the country. He certainly didn't go out of his way to let anyone know about that part of his life.

'You don't look your usual chirpy self today,' Cathy greeted him one morning in the Sixth Form common room. She was balancing a plastic cup of coffee on the top of her books. She lowered them to the table and pushed back a chair to join him.

'Who could be cheerful ploughing through this?' he scowled, and began to read:

'If this world's friends might see but once
what some poor man may often feel
glory, and gold, and crowns and thrones
they would soon quit and learn to kneel . . .'

'Poor boy,' she laughed. 'Having the metaphysical blues, are you?'

'No more than they did,' he replied. 'Old Vaughan couldn't have been more defeatist and depressing.'

'Umm, some of the poems might be a bit heavy-going,' she sympathised.

'A bit! He had a death wish! All that longing for the afterlife doesn't sound very normal to me. As if he could be sure of anything after death. Can you think of a bigger con? Get people to renounce earthly pleasures with the promise that there are greater ones to come, and then they die and there's nothing.'

'Maybe he's saying that life's greatest joy is in living on a spiritual plane.'

'But what's the point of that,' he argued, 'if you can't be sure there is one?'

'Most cultures in the world recognise the existence of a God, a creator, and try to reach him,' she reasoned.

'Perhaps it's just a question of chasing rainbows,' said Owen. 'You know, compensating for the drab lives some people live.'

'Well at least Vaughan tried to offer an alternative,' she teased. 'Now Orwell, interesting though he is, can be far more depressing: writing about decaying empires and totalitarian regimes with no hope or solutions at the end of it!'

'You wound me!' he said, clutching at his chest. 'One of the most penetrating observers of society and humanity. I think I shall have to report your remarks to Big Brother.'

Laughing, they collected their books and headed for the door. 'I'll see you later, Winston,' Cathy called after him.

Owen continued to plod along in his studies of the metaphysical poets. He had a way of accepting them on an intellectual basis, even though he vigorously resisted their spiritual quirks. When assigned an essay on Vaughan, he wound up with a thirteen-page analysis of the seventeenth-century poet and his works. His teacher praised it. 'Very detailed and searching,' she said.

Only one poet from this school earned his admiration. One day in his tutor group he quoted Marvell:

> 'See how the Orient dew
> shed from the bosom of the morn
> into the blowing roses . . .

That's quite nice, isn't it? I could have written that myself, don't you think?'

'No!' chorused Cathy and Amanda, recalling his poems.

The boys had known each other for years, but it wasn't until the Lower Sixth that they formed the 'Sardine Liberation Front'. Matthew Collins alias 'Mole' was usually in charge of beverage procurement, a position he prized judging by the look of his bedroom, full of pressure barrels and other beer-making equipment and scarcely room for a bed. That, and the Lowery garage, were regular venues for the 'society'.

In Upper Sixth, the group might be expected to spend slightly more time with schoolbooks and studying. But mayhem prevailed. They enjoyed the do-it-yourself approach to study and only talked school when they were sending up prize masters. 'Low-ewy,' they'd expertly mimic a favourite victim, 'have you been dwinking?'

Ashley Ward became another close mate. Each had his own sport (Ashley's was rugby), but they did others together: tennis, running, swimming, weights. When Ashley was dating Cathy Walker, Owen often served as father confessor. Ashley shared his Cathy-

problems with Owen and Cathy poured out her heart
to him about Ashley. It could have been a highly
difficult and even dangerous arrangement, but Owen
never gave a thing away. He was a cool customer and
never disclosed what he himself was thinking.

The Upper Sixth was like a year's tour in the
provinces before opening on the West End. Excite-
ment mounted as new events took place each month.
There was the Reading Rock Festival and trips out of
town. Owen and Ashley were kept busy with their
training and sport. Parties became more imaginative
and new alcoholic concoctions were being discovered.
Alas, teachers were making greater demands on their
students: homework and essays required more time
than in the previous year.

Owen had succeeded in clocking up eight 'O' levels
(including three As and five Bs) with the minimum of
effort and did not have quite the incentive to study
that other, less gifted students had. He knew all would
be well. Despite warnings from teachers he put only
slightly more effort into his work than in years gone
by. Nevertheless he, Cathy and Amanda were chosen
to sit for Oxbridge exams: another challenge in an
already overcrowded schedule. Luckily he enjoyed
this one and worked hard to try for a place.

Lifelong philosophies were being formed in the
classroom and students absorbed teachers' views as
unconsciously as they did those of the commercials
between episodes of *Brookside*. The teachers working
most closely with Owen's group made no secret of
their leanings. It could, of course, have been a coincidence that Owen's ideas so closely resembled theirs.
In one essay analysing a poem Owen concluded: 'I

believe the church represents the deadly snow.' His
teacher added a postscript: 'For me, the church also
represents the impotence of religion to combat death,
time and the elements. There is no warmth or relief
inside the church. . . .'

Owen's weekly training schedule included three or
four days of running, weight-lifting, skipping and
circuit training. Each Monday and Thursday he
could be seen running around local roads, the Reading University campus or the nearby woods. In rainy
or cold weather he'd still run. Perhaps only a four-mile
session on the worst days. Six or eight miles was the
summer routine. Six miles usually took thirty-five
minutes.

He did weight and circuit training three times a
week. The Lowery living room was part gymnasium:
barbells and dumbbells had a permanent home in the
corner. The set exercises included sixty press-ups, 100
sit-ups, 200 squats, ten different arm exercises and
others for legs and shoulders. Each complete set of
exercises lasted a quarter of an hour and he repeated
these four times.

Three nights a week he trained at the judo club from
6–9 pm. On those days he started off with an hour's
skipping with leg weights, perhaps in the afternoons
after school. And always during the first half-hour at
the club he went through stretching and loosening
exercises to get the blood flowing and reduce the risk
of pulled muscles. After that there was judo 'ground-
work', a forty-five-minute technique training session
with an opponent. This was the time to work on
hold-downs and armlocks and strangles. A member
would change opponents every four or five minutes

in order to keep practising every technique, not just his particular favourite. And here the coach walked back and forth between mats, analysing individual techniques in various holds.

Owen's first experience in the sport had been at the Wokingham Judo Club, for an hour on Saturday mornings. It was enough for a normal seven-year-old, but Owen from the start wasn't normal! His coach Don Rastrick worked unselfishly with the boy and after eighteen months suggested to the Lowerys that Owen was ready for a more competition-based club. So they took him to Bracknell. Here there were structured classes on different levels for all ages. Owen was scarcely nine when he entered the intermediate group and he settled down immediately to the discipline and hard work demanded by the sport. His brother Adam, almost two years his junior, followed him that same year.

Dave Lowery had started kicking a football in the back garden with his sons from the time they learned to walk. He had played on the Everton Schoolboys' team and his father before him had played for Liverpool. Eventually Dave turned to running as his sport and ran marathons with a local athletics club for years. At one time he made the qualifying time for Olympic entrants. Dave took home quite a few trophies before his son began to add his to the Lowery collection.

Dave was the ideal coach for his sons: he watched them develop, offered opportunities, threw down challenges, encouraged them to stretch themselves. Each weekend as they grew up, he took them out running on local rounds, keeping to their pace, but running yards ahead of them. Of course in the end he knew it was up to them to decide how far they wanted to go. He knew that being ambitious for them was a wasted energy unless they were ambitious for themselves. As the years passed however, he saw first Owen and then Adam take up the challenges. And every year they surprised him as that dedication and ambition grew.

Owen earned the judo yellow belt within the first year and won the green belt by the time he was ten. The following year he began running in earnest, to develop other muscles, and by the age of twelve he took up weight-training. When he began winning competitions he found it increased his ambition still more. He became fiercely competitive, and now saw life as a series of short-term and long-term goals, all of which included excelling at judo.

When the Oxbridge results were posted, there was only one successful applicant from Maiden Erlegh. Amanda Jones, Cathy Walker's friend, won a place at Oxford. Owen took it in his stride, but he knew Cathy was deeply disappointed. A few days later she received a letter from him:

Sorry you weren't happy with the results. However, I'm sure you'll more than surpass yourself at any university, whatever it is. Your great bubbly personality and your obvious talent should ensure that you are as successful as you deserve to be. Happy Christmas.

Best Wishes, OWEN

Cathy could scarcely believe this had come from Owen. It was yet another side of him she hadn't known. Often when conversations bordered on the serious they quickly joked to avoid embarrassment. Now just these few gracious words gave her another picture of her unfathomable friend.

Ashley too was surprised more than once to learn something new about his mate. Owen could always sound off eloquently about Socialism and the Utopian Society, but it wasn't just talk. What Owen longed to do, he often said, was to stay with the homeless for a while or mingle in other deprived communities to see how they lived. He wanted to understand other people's predicaments and make a tangible contribution to their lives. He lost patience with people who showed off their wealth or who pretended to be someone important. He felt the poor often had a 'raw deal' and it was up to the ordinary person, as well as the government, to help in any way he could.

During the Reading Rock Festival it was time for a blast. 'A' levels, training, judo matches and other serious issues were put away in their boxes. Deafening music, lots of booze, keeping a sharp look-out for girls, and laughs with a good mate: that was living!

A young Hell's Angel approached them one day in the midst of the festival. He had a bedraggled, desperate look about him. 'Have you anything for something to eat, mate?' he asked them.

'Sorry,' Ashley said. 'I'm down to my last quid. We're going home soon.'

The youth turned to Owen and began to explain. 'I've got to get out of here,' he said. 'I used to be a Hell's Angel, but I'm not any more. I want to get away; I want to leave Reading. This place is a bad influence on me.'

Ashley turned away, but Owen kept listening to his troubles. The youth might have been giving him a cock-and-bull story, but he couldn't be sure. In the end, Owen took him to the nearest cash machine and withdrew a fiver from his account.

'What did you do that for?' Ashley asked him after the youth had left.

'Maybe he's having me on,' Owen admitted, 'but if there's a glimmer of a chance that he's on the level it was worth it.'

There was an end-of-term party at the Lowerys'. Dave and Sybil generously disappeared for the night leaving Owen and his mates to rearrange furniture and prepare for some serious drinking. The stereo was readied for hard use, and the first guests began to arrive.

Before long the atmosphere was charged with rock music and some of the carpets were awash with beer. The noise level suggested that all were having the time of their lives. No one noticed when Owen pulled Cathy aside and motioned her upstairs.

'What's the matter?' she asked as he shut his bedroom door on the two of them.

'I don't know,' he said glumly, sitting beside her on the bed. 'I just felt like getting away for a bit.'

Cathy's guitar had followed her up the stairs and now she began to pluck at the strings. 'How about a little song?' she asked, hoping to cheer him up. He smiled as she began to play a favourite Pogues tune.

'Something weird happened last night,' he said when she had finished.

'Anything bothering you?' she asked him. It wasn't like him to open up. She decided it must have been something big to shake him up like this.

'Yeah, well, just something. I decided to pray.'

'But you don't . . .'

'I don't believe in anything,' he grinned, 'but you never know.'

Then someone rushed into the room, hooted and whistled to see them there, and the moment passed.

One day Owen sat down and penned a letter to Malcolm Collins, his long-time coach for the British Schools Judo Association.

Dear Malcolm,

I am simply writing, somewhat belatedly, to express my gratitude to you for the part you have played in arranging the six BSJA contests I have been fortunate enough to take part in. I can honestly say that all these contests have provided me with some very valuable international experience at a reasonably early age.

I know I speak for all the other team members who have benefited from your work when I tell you that I have derived a great deal of enjoyment as well as experience over the last four years. I was particularly proud to be nominated as captain during the trips to Malta and Israel as well as the home international against West Germany.

I hope you will continue to carry out your good work in the future so that many others like me will continue to benefit. Finally I hope that you are successful in your attempt to arrange a contest behind the iron curtain.

It has been a great honour to fight for the British Schools Judo Association team and especially to captain it. Thanks a lot.

Yours sincerely, Owen Lowery

P.S. The trip to Israel can't have done me any harm as I've just won the Young Men's National Trials at U-60 kg. Cheers!

It was the last great summer. 'A' levels were looming, but somehow all Owen thought about was tennis. He threw himself into the game for three or four hours at a time, trying to postpone the coming crisis. He'd worked hard at the Oxbridge exams and lost. Now his future looked blurred. Maybe he'd scrape through. If not, something would come up. It always did. He kept playing tennis and sometimes spent all day on the courts, knocking the ball around as if it were time itself being held at bay.

Chapter 2

After the 'A' level results came out Owen went fishing. He spent a peaceful afternoon down by the river at Whiteknight's Lake. He would have to alter course a bit now that he had lost Swansea. He'd been lucky to get a sports scholarship there, provisional on his results. But with only two Cs instead of the required three, he'd have to think of something else. For the moment the wisest course of action for the afternoon was to disappear and let Mum come to terms with the contents of the envelope on her own. So he headed for the river.

He wasn't the sort of person to get depressed. If something went wrong, he'd pick himself up and try again. He learned that years ago from a succession of coaches and from his father. When a fight didn't go his way, he learned to say, 'OK, I've messed that up. Now let's see how I can do better next time.' Something would turn up. Anyway, some of his mates had done no better, and some worse. Ashley, Mole and Charlie were all having to rethink their plans too.

For the next few weeks, Sybil Lowery worked quietly behind the scenes trying to find a suitable alternative for her son. A secretary at Reading University for many years, she checked offices there and finally found a place in the German department where they'd accept Owen's two Cs. His mates, too, were working out their alternatives. Ashley decided to repeat his 'A' level year. Andy, luckily, got his place at Swansea and Amanda at Hertford College, Oxford. Cathy got in at Sheffield, but she was going to delay university for a year and spend some months in Israel first.

As the summer wore on, Owen kept training and fishing and beating the life out of those tennis balls.

Owen and Ashley met one Saturday morning to go running across the Reading University campus. They started out on Wilderness Road, winding their way around Pepper Lane.

'Cathy's asked me to join her for a holiday in Snowdonia,' Ashley called over his shoulder after a long stretch of running in silence.

'Congratulations!' laughed Owen, giving his friend a poke in the arm. 'I knew you could do it!'

Ashley winced. 'With her church friends?'

'O-oh, you'd better be careful. They'll 'ave you,' Owen teased him.

'Yeah, well, that's what I was thinking. But I'd like to go. There's transport laid on from her friend's parents and with staying in hostels I could just about manage the finance. What do you say that you come along too?'

'To help hold your hymn-book? Er, no thanks. I'm not into church on holidays. They'll probably be singing "Rock of Ages" on the way up . . .' and he lapsed into an imitation of a choirboy on the rock-face.

Ashley put up with his antics for a while, but tried again. 'If you came along we could go off on our own when we felt like it.'

'You mean we could abandon ship if it became too prayer-logged?'

'We could join in when we wanted,' Ashley said, ignoring that, 'and go our own way when we didn't. What do you say?'

Owen was by this time impersonating a vicar lost in the fog, which resulted in the pair of them collapsing on the grass, doubled up and out of breath. At last they sat up and began a few stretching exercises. Ashley appealed to his friend again. Owen finally agreed, saying it was against his better judgement.

If there was one thing worse than religious people it was posh, religious people, Owen thought with a quiet groan, as he was welcomed into a very large and elegant house in Great Missenden. In the drawing room he was introduced to Cathy's friends: Philip, Guy, Julian, Sue and Emma. Owen decided that all the boys should be called Nigel and the girls Samantha.

Cathy Walker looked nervously from one group of friends to the other, wondering whether her efforts to détente in both 'camps' would prove fatal. Her Christian friends made every attempt to welcome Owen and Ashley. Questions about school, 'A' level exams, sport and other interests were met with the briefest replies.

At an early opportunity the two recalcitrant youths were off in another room sharing a private joke in which the laughter was clearly mischievous.

Cathy went in and came between them quickly.
'Now what might you two be up to?' she asked carefully. She suspected they were having a bit of fun at
her friends' expense.

'Who, us?' Wide-eyed Ashley feigned innocence.

'We were only brushing up on our speech in order to
be more presentable,' Owen said loftily, his usual
Berkshire accent mysteriously altered.

She had to grin at these two, but she didn't want to
see them get out of hand. 'Maybe if you gave them a
chance you'd find they weren't so bad after all,' she
whispered.

'Precisely our intention,' Owen said, following her.

Cathy introduces Ashley and Owen to her friends

'Absolutely,' Ashley agreed, close behind.

Two cars full of young people and camping gear set out the next morning. Owen and Ashley slid down in the back seat and winced when someone started singing songs from *Godspell*. They solved the problem by adapting the words of some rude Rugby songs to the music coming from the front seat. Everyone sang heartily.

They drove through Oswestry, said goodbye to Philip's parents in a car park on the edge of Snowdonia and walked five miles to the first hostel. They trekked through a forest, improvising on the map, and got lost looking for a lake.

'Have you seen a lake anywhere?' Owen scurried around, pretending he'd dropped it on the way.

'I heard one running a while back,' Ashley responded, as if it were trying to escape.

The next day they began their walks in earnest, pressing on through thick forests and up steep slopes. It was hot and humid at first, but as they climbed the air became crisp and the scent of the trees refreshed them. Further up in the clearings there were sun-dappled fields of wild flowers. As they climbed higher, the views over the mountain peaks were extraordinarily beautiful. Owen described the moment as 'yellow-golden'.

The weather was near perfect all week. It was soon clear that Ashley and Owen, in top form from running and other sport, were going to need a more demanding pace for the walks. They were joined by Julian who also wanted a more energetic pace. Owen at once renamed him Baldrick: no doubt due to his good-natured compliance.

Ashley and Owen on their last climb together

A pattern began to establish itself: Philip, Guy and the girls set off first, and an hour or two later the lads would follow. Often the three chose a more difficult route yet surprised the others by arriving at the destination ahead of them.

However, the Owen/Ashley travel guide for the week (otherwise called *Tales of the Unexpected*) included detours through fields of sheep, climbing over fences, sliding down wet fields and wading through waterways. They swam at any opportunity: under waterfalls, in stream or river. They'd hang their clothes on the No Swimming signs.

One day the three trudged forward confidently despite fog rolling down. Somehow they missed a road and found themselves quite lost. They sensed that their destination lay beyond the valley ahead, but to get there they'd have to cross a river. They slid down a deep ravine by the seat of their pants and then stood before the river, pondering its depths.

'I'll go,' Julian offered generously. He began to wade deeper and deeper, holding his boots high, his rolled-up jeans already below sea level. Suddenly he let out a cry. He had stepped on sharp glass.

'Thank you, Baldrick, for finding that bottle for us,' Owen called out. He and Ashley kept their boots on to make the crossing.

On the second last day the party of eight planned to walk from their hostel at Llanberis, up the Devil's Kitchen to Glyder Fawr. Their destination was the Snowdon Ranger hostel at Pen-Y-pass. The morning sky was grey, but they expected improved weather conditions later on.

The group walked to the Devil's Kitchen together, but then Owen and Ashley had the urge to try another route. Again followed by Julian, they cheerily parted from the others, leaving the compass with Philip. When the fog rolled in around them the three boys realised that their map wasn't much use to them without the compass.

'Let's just keep to the path,' said one. And they tried to do that, but somewhere in the afternoon they became disorientated and tired and they disagreed on which way they should go. Finally they looked underfoot and reached agreement: 'This footpath is made of grass.'

They stumbled along, unable to see to the right or left. They thought they saw a path, but on closer inspection it was just hard rocky ground with jagged rocks and boulders all around them. Further progress downwards became impossible. The heavy fog still hung like a curtain around them, and they measured visibility in feet.

It was late afternoon by then and they had walked for hours. They feared they may have been walking in circles. How long would it take them to get back?

'I'm going to head back up,' Julian said, and he scrambled for a safe foothold.

Owen turned next, grabbed a boulder and it came away in his hand, tumbling past him and striking Ashley on the right side. He screamed as it hit him.

'Wait!' Owen shouted. 'Don't move!'

'I can't move; I can't move!' Ashley hollered. He suddenly didn't know which way to go, and was frozen with fear. Owen realised their dangerous situation and was frightened that they could both hurtle through space to the rocks below.

Julian could only watch from above as the two lads went rigid with panic. After a quarter of an hour they slowly crept up to join Julian. The three sank to the ground together, too shocked to speak. Ashley and Owen realised that they had come very close to death and could only be grateful that they were alive.

'Perhaps we'd better stay here,' said one after a long silence.

'But it's getting dark. They'll worry,' said another.

'Then they'd call Mountain Rescue. They'll find us.'

'I reckon we should carry on.'

So they did. After an hour of walking, they came to a marsh. Ashley was so tired, he longed to sleep, but they had to move on while it was still light. Ashley sank waist-high in water, and the other two pulled him out. They were all wet through and utterly exhausted by this time.

They struggled on for hours more and eventually found themselves on a miners' trail, and then on a road on the other side of the mountain. A mini-bus stopped, and strangers gave them coffee then a lift back to their hostel at Pen-Y-pass.

On the way back, the sober-faced lads were thankful for the smallest things. They were thankful for the cup of coffee, for the seat they sat on, for the kindness of the driver. They had never come so close to death. They were glad to be alive.

Chapter 3

Andy Syed, seventeen, a direct descendent of Mohammed and winner of six major UK table-tennis tournaments, had invited Owen for a meal. Andy was also a keen snooker player and occasionally Owen and some of his mates would wander over to Andy's house of an evening to play. Ashley Ward was another who found it useful to put aside his main sport and relax with a game of snooker.

Like Ashley and Owen, Andy was highly competitive. He trained hard and played to win. In early 1986 Andy broke through to the highest level of his sport, winning senior tournaments while still a junior. He was almost certain to be selected for the forthcoming European Senior Championships.

Andy was born in the UK, but his father came from a distinguished Islamic lineage and his grandfather was the Commissioner of Police in Hyderabad, India. Andy's father, Abbas, came to London as a young man in 1961, joining Gray's Inn to study barrister law. It was only a few years later, while continuing his studies, that Abbas Syed had a vision in which God spoke personally to him. Abbas doubted the vision at first, so unworthy and sinful he felt. But hadn't he been calling out to the living God – whatever his name – to know him?

On Easter Sunday 1967, having accepted an invitation to attend a Christian service, Abbas realised that the One for whom he was searching was Jesus Christ, and that day he became his faithful follower.

As Andy entered his teens he became unusually expert at table-tennis and his coach predicted a great future for him. But Andy also shared his father's devotion to Christ and during many an evening he spent as much time encouraging friends to visit his church as he did beating them at snooker.

On Saturday night September 12, 1987 Owen cycled to Andy's house and over a meal they talked about Owen's recent holiday in Snowdonia.

'The weather couldn't have been better most days,' Owen was saying, 'and when we reached the top of Glyda Fahr, with the peaks all around us, it was like standing on top of the world.'

'You'd be surrounded by nothing but nature in the raw.'

'It was. No pollution, fumes or city noise. Brilliant!'

'Hey, that's something,' teased Andy, 'an atheist who prefers the God-made to the mere man-made. . . .'

'Well, sure, I like nature, if that's what you mean.'

'But didn't you think, as you stood there, that it couldn't be just an accident?'

'I don't know,' shrugged Owen. 'I guess I didn't think about it. Anyway, evolution is pretty well accepted by scientists.'

'Ah, but I've read a few books lately by some

scientists who believe in creation. There are many who don't swallow the idea of evolution, Owen.'

'You can't prove creation, though.'

'No,' Andy admitted, 'any more than evolution can be proved. Either way, these are scientific theories and both ought to be taught in our schools, not just evolution. Anyway, I can't see how someone with your keen mind can think that life "just happened". There's design in everything: the human body, a snowflake, a leaf, a flower.'

'There's a lot we don't understand,' Owen admitted.

'To me, design means purpose,' Andy went on. 'A man designs a chair to sit on, a shelf to hold books. You've only to study anatomy to be amazed at the function of our bones and muscles.'

'We all know about that,' Owen grinned. 'We're designed for sport, right?'

'Partly. But I think we're designed for more than that. I believe we've also got a soul or spirit, and that, I'm sure, is even more important than our body.'

'How can it be more important when we can't even see it? Besides, look around you. Most people don't take it seriously.'

'That's true. Like you, they want proof. But I believe the soul or spirit will live on – long after the body dies. We're pretty impermanent creatures, Owen.'

Owen recalled his English teacher and their studies of Vera Brittan's *Testament of Youth*. The teacher had said, 'Nothing is permanent,' and described all of life as a fleeting phase. It was a melancholy thought. What was the point of it all if everything died and went to oblivion? Owen thought again of that day in Snowdonia when he and Ashley had come so close to death. They could so easily have fallen over the side. Then what?

'You could live for seventy years, yet in the context of eternity it is still just a speck,' Andy was saying. 'But consider the possibility that the spirit is eternal. Wouldn't it be important to find out more?'

'I'll admit it does seem pointless,' Owen said, 'being on this planet for such a short time. But in that case,' he began to laugh, 'it makes sense to enjoy life as much as possible. Eat, drink and be merry, that's what I say!'

'The only trouble with that,' Andy said, 'is that one can be denied even that. Take my sport. You know I've been having trouble with my arm. . . .'

'Yeah, that's rough. I'm sorry to hear about that.'

'It's been hard to come to terms with it,' Andy admitted. 'What if I could never play again?'

'On your bike! It's not that bad?'

'I hope not. But what if it were? What if I or any other sportsman were denied the ability to keep playing? If sport was his life, he'd go mad. At least in my case it's not all there is. It's not my *life*.'

Owen thought about judo, his training, the matches, the challenges, all that he enjoyed.

'There's something much more permanent in my life,' said Andy. 'Knowing God and Jesus. Having God's Spirit in me. That's permanent.'

Owen remembered Cathy Walker's response to their English teacher. 'God is permanent, even if man isn't,' she had said firmly. And then Owen's mates had had a good snicker as the teacher produced her intellectual put-down. But Cathy wasn't deterred.

'You ought to come to the King's Church,' Andy went on. 'It's a great place. Lots of young people our age go.'

Owen thought of church as a place to hold funerals or, at best, to get married in. Perhaps later, much later. . . . 'It's not really my scene,' he said.

'If you came, you might be surprised. You'd find it wasn't at all boring.'

Owen felt like refusing, but he didn't want to hurt Andy's feelings. He was a nice bloke for a Christian. Perhaps he could go, just once. 'I'm off to St Helen's in the morning for a charity match,' said Owen, as he stood and stretched himself, getting ready to leave. 'But I'll come with you next week, OK?'

'Brilliant!' said Andy, seeing him to the door.

Chapter 4

'I must be mad getting up at this hour,' he grumbled to himself as he headed towards the bathroom. The alarm went off at 4 am and by the time he rolled out of bed he heard his mother down in the kitchen preparing a cup of tea. He washed and brushed his teeth, all the while complaining to himself for agreeing to go.

Awful long journey too, he thought, climbing into his tight and shabby jeans. He spent a few minutes searching for a lost trainer which didn't help the early-morning disposition. By this time he heard his father outdoors, opening the boot, closing the boot, getting ready for the 5 am departure. It would take almost four hours to get to St Helen's and weighing in was between 8:30 and 9:30 am.

'Cup of tea, love?' Sybil called up to him.

'No thanks.' He never had anything that early. Perhaps they'd stop halfway and he'd have a cup then. Right now all he wanted to do was to go back to bed and pull the covers up.

He picked up a few Pogues tapes to play on the way and trundled downstairs. His kit wasn't by the front door where he'd put it last night. He went out to the car and opened the boot to check that his dad had remembered.

At least there was no horrible little brother taking up half the back seat, he thought, as the car turned out of Falstaff Avenue. Adam had decided to remain in Reading and bang away at those drums of his. He stretched out across the double seat and soon drifted off to the sound of his parents chatting quietly in the front.

'Ready for a stop?' Dave called over his shoulder to the curled-up form in the back.

Owen grunted and finally looked up. 'Where are we?'

'M5. We'll be in Birmingham in about half an hour.'

'Sounds OK.' He looked at his watch. It was 6:30.

After the brief stop they climbed back into the car for the final part of the journey. Owen gradually came to life, stimulated by the cup of tea and now stirred by the sounds coming from his favourite tape. His parents endured it patiently.

At ten minutes to eight Dave turned the car off the motorway and followed the signs to St Helen's. Owen was already mentally preparing himself for the fights that would soon take place and tingling in anticipation.

It wasn't an ordinary competition taking him to St Helen's. Weeks earlier Owen and some others from his judo club had agreed to take part in a charity match up there for a lad who'd had an injury during a judo match and was now disabled. He'd only fractured his leg and dislocated his knee at the time, but later it had been discovered that particles of bone had gone into the blood vessels and his leg became gangrenous. His leg had to be amputated after that.

They jostled one another at the weigh-in, taking the mickey out of each other, hurling names back and forth.

'How's the training going?'

'Have trouble making the weight?'

'Don't forget the session next Tuesday.'

When weigh-ins were complete, they clamoured over to the food box for a cake and a sandwich and a sip of lemonade.

He was moving into the final routine now, with stretching and loosening up exercises. He went outside briefly with a club-mate to practise techniques and get some fresh air. Then they returned indoors to crowd around the control table that held the knockout sheets. Owen craned his neck over an official's shoulder to see where he was placed.

Nigel Donahue? That's strange, he thought. His long-time opponent was his equal in strength and he'd have expected to compete with him in a later round. It was no secret that they were the two best of their weight class. It was a strange pairing. Why him? Why now?

They were two minutes into the fight. Owen was feeling comfortable, confident. He picked up a small penalty for gripping Nigel around the collar too strongly. Nevertheless he was OK, under control. He moved in for a technique, but slipped forward and found himself sliding and landed on his head.

He looked up at the referee. Everything was still for

a second or two as he looked at him. His body seemed to hold in mid-air, floating, without pain. But his breath came out like the end of a sigh: 'I've broken my neck.' His eyes stayed fixed on the referee.

Suddenly there was commotion all around him, although within his floating cocoon he lay perfectly still. St John's Ambulance men rushed forward. It looked as if they were lifting him up, but he could not feel their hands. There was a searing pain in his neck that shot through his head, rushing and whistling like a bitter wind through a crack in the door.

His mother's face leaned over him, loving, smiling. Her hand came out to his hair. His father, frowning, anxious, pushed past others who were looking on. He wanted to reach out and take his mother's hand, but then looked down to see she had already caught his fingers in her own.

Sybil sat by her son in the ambulance as it raced along unfamiliar streets to the nearest hospital. She wondered whether he'd been winded, as he seemed to have trouble breathing and the attendant fed him oxygen to help. And he lay there, so still . . .

He wasn't still for a moment in those early years. At first she thought it was the normal rough and tumble of being a seven-year-old boy. This was their firstborn and she, an only child, had no close knowledge of what to expect of a boy. He and his friends were always getting into scrapes, it's true. Perhaps, because he was a bit smaller than the others, he thought he'd have to be tougher to catch up. He and his friend Simon Lambourne were always at it! Then they'd make up and go off to the river together.

'I'm putting him down for judo,' Simon's mother announced one day over a cup of tea. She too was getting worn out by her son's limitless energy.

'That's not a bad idea,' agreed Sybil, willing to try anything to work some of that aggression out of Owen's system. She accompanied the Lambournes to the judo club days later.

Within a few weeks at the judo club, Sybil and Dave knew it was just what their son needed. A year or two earlier they'd tried him at Cubs and at first he was enthusiastic. Then he seemed to get impatient: 'Can I do this badge? Why can't I take another one?' and his little body didn't want to wait to follow the normal routine laid out for the lads. Finally, when his parents said he needn't go any more, he threw his cap up in the air and gave a yell.

He kept up with his swimming lessons, though, and won a gold medal at the age of ten for personal survival achievement. In later years he continued to swim vigorously, but more for leisure or for relaxation after judo sessions. And for eight years he played for various local football teams: first the Shinfield Rangers, then Bracknell Boys and the Earley Eagles. Always running, playing, competing; always on the go.

The ambulance turned up the ramp into the Casualty Department and quickly the back doors were opened and a team of people rushed forward.

'Where are we?' Sybil leaned towards the driver.

'Whiston Hospital, love,' he said.

Sybil looked down at Owen, and he spoke slowly. 'I can't move my arms or legs.'

Then staff moved between them and slid him out of

Owen just before the St Helen's match

the ambulance and into the hospital. Sybil hurried to keep up with her son whose body was now swept along on a chilling tide of activity over which she had no control. Dave found a parking place and rushed to her side.

During the next hours their anxiety increased. They waited as near to their son's stretcher as they were allowed, but they were none the wiser for it. Doctors rushed to and fro, X-rays were taken, staff conversed in incomprehensible medical jargon. Dave and Sybil often felt in the way, unnecessary obstacles, as nurses jostled around them. Finally a doctor approached them.

'We're going to have to do an operation on Owen,'

he said. 'He's displaced two bones in his neck. This has caused us concern for his breathing. I've been in touch with the Southport Promenade Hospital and the consultant there thought he'd be safer on a ventilator.'

These words were vaguely reassuring, since neither parent understood the awesome implications. 'Can we see him?' was all Sybil could think of to say.

Owen lay on a trolley, a sheet covering his body. The only evidence that something was amiss was his judo suit lying in cut-up shreds on a nearby chair. Otherwise, Sybil thought, he looked quite peaceful. Surely it couldn't be so very bad?

She reached out to touch his arm. 'You'll be all right,' she said.

Owen's breathing was shallow, but he said, 'I love you, Mum.'

Dave too was having a struggle in his chest and for the life of him couldn't get a word out. He just looked down at his son, devastated.

When Owen was wheeled into surgery, Sybil and Dave decided to phone Adam in Reading. 'I think you'd better come up,' Sybil said into the phone.

'Why?'

'Owen has had a fall on the mat, and has hurt his neck.'

'He's . . . not going to die?'

'He could.'

They arranged for Adam to borrow money from a neighbour and take the next train from Reading which would get into Liverpool at midnight. Dave would be there to meet him.

Dave climbed into the car outside Whiston Hospital and fastened his seatbelt. He turned the key and began to move out, but his mind didn't seem to be functioning properly. It kept coming in waves, the feeling of disbelief that it had happened, and disbelief of what the doctors had hinted at. How could he trust them? How could they know what was wrong, anyway? And if they did know, how could he be sure they were telling it like it was? What if it was worse than they were saying? Surely it might be less serious? Ah, they didn't know what a tough lad they were dealing with!

Dave drove mechanically, knowing the way to Liverpool – familiar territory from his youth. He just couldn't believe it. To think that Owen might have been playing in another competition down South today if the organisers hadn't cancelled. He would never have come to St Helen's.

You couldn't blame judo, though. It could have happened anywhere; in a car or any other sport.

He had always tried to support the boys, whatever they were interested in. He gave them time, finance or transport whenever they needed it. He liked to run with them or kick a football. He wasn't the sort of person who talked a lot, who believed in leading with words. Some folk do a lot of talking and nothing else. He believed in doing a job, not talking about it. You lead by example, by what you do. That's what's important.

Oh, he thought, to think of the geezers kicking around the country getting away with all sorts of villainy! Does this sort of thing happen to them?

'What exactly happened?' was the first thing Adam asked as he hurried to join his father.

'They say he's broken his neck.'

'So that's what it is!' Adam was stunned, as if he'd been winded.

The Stanmore neurosurgeon at Whiston had told Dave point-blank: 'I'm afraid he'll be in a wheelchair for the rest of his life.'

'But it won't be permanent or anything, will it?' Adam was saying now.

'We hope not,' Dave said. 'We'll have to wait and see. The doctors won't tell us anything at the moment.'

When father and son arrived it was well past midnight and Owen had been taken from surgery into the Intensive Care Ward. The sister allowed them in for a brief visit.

Adam stared wide-eyed at the figure lying on the high hospital bed. His live-wire older brother who could do anything, who was always a winner, whom he'd tussled with only the day before, now close to death? It couldn't be! It was impossible! Not Owen!

There were tubes everywhere. One went into Owen's arm, connected to a drip strung up on a rack. Another appeared from under his bedclothes and hung to a waste bottle on the floor. Protruding from Owen's neck was a great plastic pipe like a vacuum cleaner attachment, strung up to a whirring bellows-type machine behind him. And worst of all, over his head, a fearsome-looking metal 'halo' with clamps that seemed to disappear into his skull. Suddenly Adam felt rather sick. But Owen's eyes were upon him, and he mustn't let on. Adam smiled and said, 'How are you, mate? How do you feel? Are you OK?'

Owen moved his lips, but nothing came out. With horror Adam realised that he couldn't speak. He leaned over to take his brother's hand, but it lay still and unresponsive on the sheet. Only Owen's eyes could make contact, and tell him that he was glad Adam had come.

Adam stood there, silently willing his brother to make it, to pull through.

Chapter 5

Cathy Walker was on holiday in France, touring with her family. Before many days had passed she longed to speak to Ashley back at home. 'You don't sound very happy to hear from me,' she said.

'It's not that . . .'

'Is something wrong?'

'Haven't you seen the newspapers?' he said desperately.

'I'm in France, you know!' she laughed. 'What is it?'

'It's Owen . . .'

She had never heard him sound so broken before. No, no; it couldn't be. . . . 'He's not dead?'

'No, but . . .'

'Oh, do tell me!'

'It was a judo accident. He's broken his neck . . .'

Cathy's first feeling was one of relief. Thank God he's not dead, she prayed.

'. . . but he's paralysed,' she heard over the phone. It was a terrible word to hear. One of those words that evokes fear and dread. No doubt Ashley was still in shock. She knew he had been closer to Owen than any of his other mates this past year and that the news would have knocked him for six. But there within her, even now, was a comfort, a hope. God cared, she thought fiercely. He would do something! When she had finished the call she dropped to the grass outside the phone kiosk and sat there, hugging her knees. She pressed her forehead against her knees, praying for Owen. What else in the world was there?

After a moment she looked up and thought of Ashley. He'd be suffering in a different way. She knew he'd not be seeking refuge in prayer. He'd be thinking that it was all so useless, so unfair. Where would he find his comfort? All those months he had dutifully attended church with her, he hadn't really become involved in the way she'd hoped he would. Would he think of that now? Would he begin to understand? Or would he be tempted to say: 'So much for your God now! Look what he's done to Owen!'

Dot and Derek Ogden were on the beach in the Canary Islands when they opened a *Daily Mirror* and saw Owen's face staring at them. The news that accompanied it sent them rushing to the nearest phone to see if it could be true. They called their friends the Donahues and discovered that it was Nigel Donahue who had faced Owen on the mat during that fateful moment.

The Ogdens and Donahues, friends for years, were of good solid Lancashire stock with sons roughly the same age who lived for judo. They were forever bumping into each other at matches and competitions locally and throughout the country. And although the lads often competed with each other, the friendships remained firm.

To both couples Owen had been someone very special. They knew his parents too. Owen was a lad who was going somewhere and when his name appeared on a list you could bet it was going to be a good match.

Derek Ogden had decided that at a meet in Stockton in 1979. 'Our David wer' best in t'Northwest,' Derek told some friends later. 'I watched him struggling with this blond boy from down South. And even though our son wer' a green belt at the time and twelve months older, why, this ten-year-old beat him! And he wer' only an orange belt then! I said: "Let's make a note of that lad," and went over t'board. His name wer' Lowery. Owen Lowery.'

When the dreaded news was confirmed the Ogdens were devastated. Initially, they couldn't resist thinking it might have been their David lying in hospital fighting for his life. Then they thought of Sybil and Dave and how this must be tearing them apart. The last three days of the holiday were sober ones. They flew home, plonked their cases down in the hall and headed straight for Southport Promenade where Owen had been transferred.

'At first you just stood ther',' Derek explained. 'Ther' wer' nothing you could say. And he couldn't talk. You just wanted to be wi' him.'

Sybil and Dave were given a room in the nursing home. They arrived in the ward early one morning while the doctors were doing their rounds. A nurse told Sybil they were about to wash her son and change his dressings. Maybe they'd like to wait in the day-room?

It was a forlorn looking place, with shabby chairs, an old TV set and a table stuck in the middle. An old man was asleep in the corner. Soon two paraplegics wheeled themselves in, followed by a third. One was surprisingly proficient in wheelchair-obics, twirling around and challenging the others to do the same. He then drove the table nearer to the window to allow more space for the three wheelchairs. This woke the old man who shuffled out. The young patients pulled out cigarettes, laughing about the nurses who would be sure to rush in to extinguish them. Some ribald jokes were exchanged.

Sybil looked at the strong, muscular arms on the lads; from the waist up they looked perfectly normal. Somehow this cheered her. She imagined each as bedridden, like Owen, a short time ago. Perhaps they too had been immobilised with headclamps and weights, had spent weeks whispering above the drone of the ventilator, had been fed by other hands. Now they seemed cheerful, almost normal. Soon Owen will be like that too, she thought.

Chapter 6

'Hello, Owen.' The face was his mother's, pale, smiling, but then it turned into his Aunt Hilda's and he was being rushed back, sirens blaring, to Shinfield, along that rocky, unsurfaced road beyond Seymour Avenue on the way to the stream. He was cycling madly now, trying to reach the stream where Adam and Uncle Stan would be waiting for him. They had promised to help him look for frogs today. He tried to hurry, tried to pedal faster, but he couldn't make any progress. He couldn't get beyond the orchard where last summer they'd crept through the hole in the wire fence to scrump all those apples. Why couldn't he go faster? Maybe they wouldn't wait. . . .

Summers were the best. He and Adam weren't old enough to fish, but they loved to collect ants and spiders and beetles, and stones and frogs. There were apple fights with the other kids, and walks to a nearby farm where he played hide and seek with the goat tethered in the front garden. Uncle Stan was always out shooting something or other and when he got caught shooting that Canadian goose Aunt Hilda said that pretty soon the cows would start disappearing.

'Can you hear me, love?' He managed with great effort to open his eyes and his mum was there again. She seemed much taller somehow, looking down on him from a great height. Her eyes looked worried. Was she cross? Perhaps he shouldn't have hidden in Peter's old stock car behind the shed when she called him for dinner. Now he'd get it good and proper from his dad.

'It's only the drugs,' someone said, a voice he couldn't recognise. In fact, it seemed he'd heard that voice, and others, say that over and over since this all began. But he couldn't quite figure what 'this' was, however hard he tried. It was Shinfield, that's where it began. Was he travelling to Shinfield? Or was he leaving it? That last long summer he was bouncing along the stony path on his bike, past the cornfields and through the orchard, but somewhere someone was calling him again. He didn't mean to be quiet and not answer. His eyes were heavy again and he couldn't open them. He tried to call out: I'm here, I'm here; I hear you. But no sound came out.

Part of the time he knew what had happened and that he was in hospital. But then he was taken away, against his will, into a massive room with several tiers of bunk beds around the walls. People came in and stopped to look at him and whisper. He was on a top bunk, yet somehow friends, judo coaches and his mum and dad all managed to look down on him. At last he understood – they were on the ceiling and that's why they could look down from a height.

In one corner of the great room an Indian family lived on the ceiling. They whispered together too and looked at him. There was eerie Asian music coming from somewhere and then, like sounds rising from the darkness, the tones turned ominous and evil. Perhaps someone was taking jewellery off those in the corner. The evil presence in the room was getting closer and closer.

His father's face bent over him and around his neck hung a large gold necklace. Why had he taken it? Owen knew it was connected with some Indian ritual and that it was dangerous to have stolen it. He was sure to get into trouble for that!

And all the while the cloud-like ceiling was alternately raised and lowered and people slid up and down on ropes that turned into little sticks that came closer and closer and were finally thrust into his mouth.

'It's up again,' the nurse said, turning away.

'Is it serious?' Sybil asked.

'No, it's just the drugs,' Owen heard again, but this time it sounded as if it were spoken slowly, mournfully, and then high-pitched, speeding out of control.

Those people were very evil indeed. They used a set of remote control fish hooks to manipulate the others trapped in the bunk beds. By twiddling the control box wires they could raise or lower men whenever they wished. One poor soul was sucked up into the ceiling. The awful thing was that heavy objects too, were attached to wires and these loomed over him, threatening to crush him or slice him in two.

Owen tried to tell his mother to beware of the ceiling, to help prevent the bicycles and rolling pins from crushing him. He looked up at the ceiling and then at her, panic filling his eyes. He tried to whisper what was wrong, but the whirr of the machines all around him drowned him out.

'What's the matter, love? Was it a nightmare?' Sybil leaned over and stroked his damp forehead. He looked very frightened and kept scowling at the ceiling.

'There . . .' he whispered, looking up.

'There's nothing there, love,' she told him. 'It was just a bad dream.'

'No . . .' he whispered, wanting her to believe him. He knew what he saw. There was danger up there. The next one could kill him. Some other friends came close and looked at him and then at the ceiling, and shook their heads. They didn't believe him either.

Then the terrorists began in earnest. They were big military types, utterly ruthless. They held everyone hostage, with some forced to stand against the walls and others, like himself, lying flat on their backs. They took one nurse outside and sliced her to pieces in a field. One took photos of her and they brought the slides into the room, showing her mutilated and bloodied corpse lying in the long grass. They stuck them in front of his face as if to say: 'You're next.'

One of the doctors was in league with the terrorists: a big, fleshy, cruel man. He took a large sharp knife and sliced Owen's body and legs in long strips. The terrorists warned him that if he yelled they'd not sew him back up. It was a test, of course. Owen didn't yell even once, and they allowed a staff member to stitch him up again.

The terrors kept coming in waves. He'd be within a hair's breadth of death and would just manage to escape. But then something even more horrifying would grip him and he'd fear this was the end.

The murderers were closing in now. They boarded up the ceiling with plywood and began to set fire to it. 'Go to sleep,' someone said, and he knew that if he did he'd never wake up again. He smelled the smoke in his nostrils and could do nothing to stop the inevitable. So this is how it is. . . .

Somehow the next morning the fire had been extinguished, but the danger wasn't passed. He had to tell his dad about the car bombs. There could be one under their car!

Dave Lowery came in shortly afterwards with a large card on which he had written the alphabet. He slid his finger along the letters of the alphabet, watching his son to see which letter would cause Owen to whisper 'yes'. Finally he collected the letters for CAR BOMB. What did that mean? Owen turned his eyes to the door. He was telling him to check the car!

'Is that what you want?' Dave asked. 'You want me to check it out?'

'Yes,' Owen whispered, relieved that he was finally understood.

'But Owen, it was just a nightmare. You've had some awful dreams, but you're OK now. There's nothing out there.'

Owen looked so distressed, so threatened, that nothing would dissuade him. Finally Dave agreed to go in order to put his son's mind at ease.

The doctors had told Sybil and Dave that the drugs were needed to immobilise Owen's head and neck, to ensure that he kept perfectly still during these critical first days. They had also warned them that the medication caused hallucinations in some cases. Standing there in the green-painted corridor, listening to his matter-of-fact explanation they might have been discussing how to make a cup of tea.

During the last few days it had been worse than death for Dave to watch his son clamped down, hooked up, filled with tubes, paralysed and unable to speak. As if that weren't enough, the boy was being mentally tortured with dreams and hallucinations. How much more did he have to endure? What kind of a God – if there was a God – would let this happen?

Sybil feared for Owen's sanity. The doctors could be casual about it all and describe the phenomenon as temporary, but how could they know? How could they be sure? Lately, even when awake, even when they were chatting about home or Adam's studies, Owen would indicate there were people or animals or fish coming from the ceiling. It seemed like paranoia. Were they going to have to bear this cross too?

Owen's school chum Mole arrived one afternoon having driven up from Reading as soon as he could. Mole looked down at his friend and shuddered. Owen was sleeping peacefully at the time, and Mole was grateful for the chance to take it all in without Owen's eyes upon him. He couldn't believe this had happened, only days after they had laughed and caroused together.

Later Owen awoke. He smiled a greeting, but Mole hadn't recovered sufficiently yet and all he could think of to say was: 'You look like a Martian with all that antennae. We'll just have to paint you green.'

Then he was horrified at the way it had come out. But Owen laughed. He seemed to enjoy it.

Malcolm Collins, Birmingham schoolteacher and coach of the British Schools Judo team, came to visit. He spent a quarter of an hour at Owen's bedside, trying to hold a one-sided conversation, trying to keep it light, when all the time he felt like bursting. Afterwards, talking to friends back in the corridor, he could let it out.

'He was an officer and a gentleman!' Malcolm said brokenly. 'He was such a good ambassador! The times he represented Britain as captain, he was so conscientious.

'Owen always set an example. He was never nasty, never grumbled. He wanted to win, and he did! But above all, he was a gentleman. With Owen you could say: "Have the team here at 1.30," and you could depend upon it they'd be there. That's the sort of lad he was.

'We travelled to Israel, Germany and Holland with the team so I saw him in every type of situation. And of course I'd known him since he was twelve when we first worked together. What potential he had in him then! He developed his skill and technique over the years and had what it takes to get to the Olympics.

'I've kept a letter he wrote to me last year when he was only seventeen. He thanked me for the help I'd given him. He spoke of the honour it was to have represented his country. What a letter it was! No one's ever done that to me before.'

And then he stopped and shook his head, remembering. 'Oh, it's just terrible, terrible.'

The nightmares returned. Owen was back at his old judo club, Pinewood. Somehow two chow dogs got onto the mats and one, a big black one, charged towards Owen. He went to turn and run away, but he couldn't move. He was pinned down on the mat, but no one could help him, no one could save him from what was happening. He and Ashley were climbing up a rock-face, but they could see neither ahead nor behind them. It was like the edge of the world and if they slipped they'd be sucked out into space. Then the earth turned and he was on his head and he couldn't feel his fingers any more. He was losing his grip and he was falling. . . .

He awoke in a panic, fearing he was dropping through space. Then he remembered where he was. 'I'm safe!' he wanted to cry out, grateful to be in hospital. Suddenly he felt that the fog had lifted, that he could think clearly again. The torments he'd experienced all those days were so horrific that finding himself in the Intensive Care Ward was like a reprieve from the hangman's noose. He could only be thankful and relieved.

Dave perfected his alphabet chart and communications improved. On a new board he lined the letters into four rows and when Owen searched for a new letter Dave would ask first: 'Is it in Row I? Row 2? Row 3? Row 4?' It eliminated the need to run through the entire alphabet each time.

'H A L L U C I N -' Owen spelled out, using his father's finger.

'Hallucinations?' Dave offered. 'We knew. The doctors said it might happen. It must have been awful.'

Owen screwed up his eyes to agree.

'It's all over now,' Dave said.

Chapter 7

Sybil was reading to Owen one day and a nurse interrupted. 'Mrs Lowery, the consultant would like to have a word.'

Sybil put the book down on the cabinet, already piled high with tubes and dressings, Ribena bottles, cards and letters from well-wishers. She'd been reading a long while so it felt good to get up and move around. She wiggled her shoulders to relax, then looked down at Owen, immobile. His eyes followed her and he smiled.

Sybil sat down opposite the doctor, grateful for a friendly face in the midst of confusion.

'Mrs Lowery, you know Owen's had a chest infection?'

'Yes, but it will get better, won't it?'

'Well, yes; that's not really a problem. That can be sorted out.'

Sybil smiled, waiting for him to continue.

'It's the diaphragm. I'm afraid it's not working.'

'That's why he's been on a ventilator?'

'That's right.'

'But he was breathing in the beginning. I mean, after the accident . . . he wasn't on the ventilator right away.'

'Yes, but there was subsequent damage to the diaphragm. He really can't function without it now.'

'You mean, for a while?'

'I mean always, Mrs Lowery. For the rest of his life.'

Sybil felt a tightness in her own throat now; breathing was difficult in her own body too.

'It's been a very severe injury, you see. These young men propelling themselves in wheelchairs down the corridor are the lucky ones. Their injuries might be to the fifth or sixth vertebrae. They'll be paralysed from the waist downwards, but they'll have no breathing problems and will have full use of their arms. In many cases they'll be very fit from the waist up, and will have strong arm muscles. Some will even be able to engage in sport.'

Sybil recalled the youths in the TV room doing wheelies, joking and smoking together. The lucky ones; injured 'only' at the fifth vertebra. The doctor spoke on, the words too cruel to absorb, though he meant to be comforting.

She returned to Owen's room, but the curtains were closed. The nurses were bustling about behind the brightly flowered material and she sensed by the familiar noises that they were changing the dressings and clearing out his trachea tube. She walked up and down the hall for a few moments and then stood in front of a notice-board filled with various notices and letters about spinal injuries games, contests and out-ings. Just like the judo world, she thought, a whole new fraternity of sportsmen and parents travelling up and down the motorways to compete and get medals. But for 'judo' read 'spinal injuries'.

The curtains parted and the blue eyes looked up at her, calm, trusting.

'Want me to read again, love?'

'Yes,' he whispered, still smiling.

Fred Drake, the old fellow in the next bed, put down his magazine and listened. She'd have to read a bit louder if he was to hear it all. The other noise in the ward didn't leave much room for her soft voice.

Dave's face appeared round the curtain. She wanted to rush out there and then to unburden the distressing news. But Owen mustn't get upset or notice her worry. 'How are things?' Dave asked, looking down at his son.

'Not too bad,' Owen motioned with his lips.

Sybil closed the book and tucked it between the water jug and the Kleenex box. Fred Drake turned back to his magazine. Dave pulled up a red plastic chair, trying to get close to the bed without disturbing the tubes and wires which surrounded it.

'Traffic was awful today,' he began.

After half an hour, Sybil got up from the other side of the bed and put on her jacket. 'I think I'll take a walk,' she said to Dave. 'Want to come with me?'

Something in her expression made him say casually, 'Might as well.'

She didn't speak as they walked down the long corridors to the front entrance. They went out into the bracing September air. The sea breeze was as frisky as usual, the cold wind like a firm hand telling her to mind.

The last of the holidaymakers were still trying to squeeze a few more days of summer from the resort. Young families, couples young and old, wandered around the boating lake opposite the hospital. Sybil and Dave found an empty bench and sat down. 'He's going to die,' she said without looking at him.

Dave heard the words he'd been thinking himself over the last few days. But now it was out, the worst no longer hidden.

Sybil told him about the consultant and about the diaphragm. She mentioned the lads in the dayroom, the 'lucky' ones. For a while they sat there together, too stunned to speak. Finally she felt herself gathering strength for another go. They got up off the bench, dodged some laughing, running children, waited for a stream of cars to pass, and crossed the street to the large, turreted Victorian building.

Cathy Walker and Amanda Jones met up in Liverpool and took the train to Southport the first week they could get away. Mole, who had visited a week or two earlier, had tried to prepare them. 'It's a pretty frightening sight,' he said. 'His head is clamped back with weights so you'll have to stretch to let him get a good look at you. And he can't talk.'

The girls wondered what kind of a conversation they could hold with him if he couldn't respond. Would they just have to rattle on to each other, as if he weren't there?

'Remember how he used to clown in Mrs Harvey's class?' Cathy asked as the train sped northwards.

'The way he'd nick her biscuits out of the cupboard!' Amanda reminded her.

'And that crazy way he'd open the window like a robot,' Cathy laughed.

'Do you remember at the end of term, when he came into the common room so drunk and dazed. . . .'

'*Low-ewy, have you been dwinking?*' they finished together noisily.

'Good old Owen,' Cathy said after they had collected their thoughts. 'They won't keep him down.' She knew about the respirator, and couldn't imagine he'd put up with that longer than he had to.

They took a taxi from the train station and drove along the front. There was a circus atmosphere, with flags flying and plenty of people about. You almost expected to see the illuminations glittering away, another Blackpool. As they turned the corner, there it stood: a gingerbread sort of building, all red-tiled and green-roofed with turrets and gables, a sand-castle built by the sea. But inside it was pure hospital: long corridors, wheelchairs, beds and machinery; all serious business. The girls began to feel nervous.

Then they saw him. He looked out of the corner of his eye as they approached, and his eyes followed them to the other side of the bed. Apart from the clamps, Cathy reasoned, he didn't look all that different. He didn't have a shirt on, and the sheet had slipped to show his strong muscular shoulders, still firm from years of training. Cathy looked at those muscles and thought of his energy, and her mind refused to take in the extent of his injury.

'I brought you something,' Cathy said, pulling a parcel out of her shoulder bag. 'One of my masterpieces.' She pulled off the brown paper and held it near him. It was a framed sketch of Owen, done in pencil from a Snowdonia photograph.

'It's beautiful,' Sybil exclaimed. 'You're quite professional! Isn't it good, Owen?' she asked him, and he mouthed 'yes'.

Dave came in with Derek and Dot Ogden and all were introduced. Adam was also there, standing next to his brother's bed. He seemed quite good at reading Owen's lips and was assigned the role of translator when a reply was called for.

Soon they were all talking cheerfully about a party Adam had been to the night before, and about his next match in a fortnight.

'You're going to Sheffield in September, aren't you? What will you be doing before then?' Sybil asked Cathy.

'I'm off to Israel in the New Year to work in a hostel for five months. It will give me a good chance to see something of the country.'

'What made you decide to work in Stoke until then?' Dave asked.

'My uncle has a business there, and said I could stay with them too. It saves me a lot of money! And contrary to what some people think,' she laughed, 'Stoke is a great place to live!'

'Like Liverpool, where I come from,' said Dave.

'That's right,' Cathy agreed. 'I've been surprised by the people. I think they're much friendlier up North.'

'Hear, hear,' agreed Derek, who decided there was some hope for this southern lass.

The girls ate chips walking along the seafront, although the chill winds reminded them that it was October. They went back in the evening and more light-hearted conversation continued around the bed until it was time to leave. The girls were given a room upstairs, with a neon ceiling light, two beds and an aluminium side table.

The following day they returned to the Intensive Care Ward, standing by the bed, greeting new faces. Cathy spent some time reading the newspaper to Owen, although most of the news was grim. There were few exceptions.

They had been with him for two days and yet it still seemed unreal, Cathy thought on her way back to Stoke. It was hard to think of that clamped and drained, still and silent form as her old pal Owen. Or was this a bit of self-delusion to keep her from seeing the real horror of it all?

After that weekend she was haunted by the memory of the young 'stranger'. She forced her mind to concentrate on God's mercy in sparing his life, and the possibility that he might make something good come out of it all. The Christian's hope was certainly more tangible than secular optimism, the sort of wishful thinking that says: 'Oh you'll see, he'll be right as rain in no time at all.'

She knew that was the ultimate in self-delusion. If there was a God who cared (and she knew there was) then he cared about Owen. He had to do something!

'Your son is stable now; he's out of danger,' the consultant, Mr Krishnan, announced to Sybil and

Dave after calling them into his office. It was the third weekend since the accident.

This was the first piece of good news the Lowerys had received since that day in St Helen's. The last time they had spoken together, Mr Krishnan had given them the full, grim picture: 'He'll be dependent on the ventilator for the rest of his life. He'll have no movement. And there's the possibility that he could die at any point.'

During those first weeks Owen was too critically ill for either of them to consider returning to work. They stayed by his bedside all hours of the day and night, even when Owen was drugged and in another world. A few times Dave drove down to Reading to look in on Adam, who had to return to school, and to take care of family and business matters. But for the most part their lives were suspended in unreality. The unfamiliar surroundings disorientated them; they ate or slept at odd hours; the long hospital corridors were like a tunnel from which they couldn't emerge.

Now that Owen had stabilised it was time for Dave to return to work. Sybil remained in Southport, in the room at the hospital, even though she knew it would be a blessed relief to return to her job in Reading, to keep her mind occupied with routine chores. She decided to go back in a week or two if he felt a bit stronger then.

During the long days spent at the hospital Sybil got to know other patients in the Intensive Care Ward and the tragedies that had brought them there. Walking along the corridors day after day, mingling with patients and staff, was like taking a crash course in nursing, social welfare, medical technology and anatomy. She was learning fast about the spinal cord in particular. She began to realise that in this age of organ transplants and artificial parts, the spinal cord remains the major thread of life in the human being and it cannot be repaired. When one's spinal cord is severed the damage is irreversible.

Sybil began to read about the central nervous system and the spinal cord, that mainline of communication between the brain and the body, threaded through a series of bones (vertebrae) forming the spine. One nurse described to her the four groups of vertebrae and the result of damage at different levels. Injury to the spinal cord at cervical level affected the diaphragm, arms, hands and fingers, at thoracic level the chest and abdominal muscles, at the lumbar level the leg muscles and at sacral level the bowel and bladder.

The nurse explained that one who broke his back would be paralysed from the chest or waist downwards, with little or no feeling in the lower limbs and lower trunk. This was called paraplegia. The higher up the injury, the more extensive the loss of movement and feeling. A broken neck affected the arms and hands as well, known as quadriplegia (or tetraplegia).

Sybil learned that Owen's injury was between the second and third cervical vertebrae: one of the highest points of damage to the spine and one which was often fatal.

Chapter 8

When Owen came to after that last horrific halluci-nation, and found himself safe and alive, lying on a hospital bed, he was grateful. He had always thought you didn't survive a broken neck. But he had!

With a mind now clear he assessed the situation. He had four drips in or out of his body, traction and weights on his head, a balloon-type breathing device that didn't permit him to speak. The above was all temporary. His first and immediate goal was to get rid of them!

The staff had been as helpful as possible. From his first conscious moments they had explained what had happened and what was about to happen. They didn't leave him in the dark.

'If you broke your leg,' the Indian Dr Sony said, 'it would be in plaster to keep it still. This traction is like a head-to-toe plaster; it serves the same purpose. You'll have to stay like that for six weeks, then it comes off.'

A nurse explained about the balloon-cuff coming from his tracheotomy opening. 'That will have to stay there for about six weeks, then we'll exchange it for another and you can talk again.'

The staff assured him that he'd be up in a wheel-chair before his birthday in November. Perhaps six or seven weeks more to remain in bed.

Six weeks! When he was a lad in Shinfield, on summer holidays, six weeks went on forever. He thought of the first vole he saw: such a tiny thing, the thrill of a new discovery; Uncle Stan playing hide and seek with that crazy brown-and-white goat, and how he used to bend down and give the goat a 'piggy-back' around the garden; those great dinners from Aunt Hilda, and the pies with tons of pastry on them.

He thought of all the fights he had had with Adam about stupid things like what to watch on the telly. They'd roll about, punching each other, but they broke up pretty quickly, Owen remembered, smiling inwardly. Adam would run off looking for his mum.

It was a different story when they were out together playing football, running around the fields, leaping over the huge nettle beds on the way to the river looking for fish. Just let some other kid try anything with Adam – he'd soon get belted.

When he was eight life got a bit more serious, with all the training. Don Werner put him on the right track. He wasn't the sort to be satisfied with just taking part and losing graciously. Owen soon cap-tured the same spirit from his judo coach; there was no point in training to lose. Don Werner instilled in him a fierce desire to win at all costs. You find your op-ponent's weak points and you hammer home at them. Owen's singlemindedness, his cussed determination, grew each year. He often got out on that mat resolving to win simply because there were blokes there who didn't want him to. There was nothing that could make him more awkward and aggressive than the thought of people wanting him to lose.

Sometimes he did lose of course, and he'd go off and sulk quietly for a while, and then make sure he didn't lose to the same bloke the next time. He'd never tell anyone about it, but the resolve would grow and he'd train more fiercely than before.

He wasn't negative about it. He didn't believe in being negative. He never looked back. No point in being miserable when something's gone wrong. No point in saying 'if only' or 'what if?'. That to his way of thinking was just a waste of precious time. We're given only so many years and it's daft to spend them on regrets. You go on and salvage what you can.

He thought of Geoffrey Dickson, his old training partner when he was ten. Geoff was just twelve then and won the National Juniors championship. He gave Owen the idea of training hard and fast, of attacking relentlessly. He was very strong mentally on the mat. 'Don't let up,' he'd tell him.

He recalled those 'A' level results, the botch he'd made of them. And how he'd gone fishing to clear the air. When something went wrong he'd close up that box and open another – have a walk around town, see some mates, play tennis. After a good, hard session of something else he could return to the problem refreshed and tackle it again. And win next time around.

The difficulty with not being able to talk was that there were jokes welling up inside him that couldn't come out. It was real torture for such a chatty sort of person. He had to be satisfied with talking to himself sometimes. He spent a lot of time day-dreaming about fishing.

Q: Doesn't that upset you?
A: Not at all, I always catch something!

He became an expert on routines. He quickly learned when his own visitors were likely to come and when other patients' visitors were due. He told the time by the sound of Billy's radio or Fred's telly. He knew all the day's programmes by heart. He knew the nurses' shifts and how many tablets each patient was given at night and other rather more private details.

Adam spent hours at his bedside. Usually a lad of few words (like their dad) his brother now found himself having to conduct 100% of the conversation. He managed surprisingly well.

'Remember that fancy dress party in Ascot?' Adam said one Saturday morning. 'With Nick and Ashley?'

Owen certainly did. He'd gone as a flasher, with the minimum of attire under a big dirty raincoat. Trouble was, it was a posh crowd. Can't think why we were ever invited, Owen grinned inwardly. There were Porches out front with yuppies talking about their mummys and daddys. That sort of atmosphere always put Owen on his worst behaviour. He was later sent home in disgrace.

Adam grinned. 'They never asked you back again! And how about that party you threw with Dave, Charlie, Mole and Andy?'

The original Green Party, Owen thought.

'You had bright green punch made from a hideous

concoction of creme de menthe, whisky, brandy and sherry. The problem was what it did to the carpet.'

Owen recalled a whitish carpet with flowers on it. After that night, there were random 'leaves' in green.

'At least at the next party we chose a house where the carpets were a Guinness-coloured brown.'

Adam knew by the little smirk appearing at the corner of Owen's mouth that he'd already been thinking about that one.

Owen thought of the future on two levels. He had always lived with goals in mind: immediate ones and future ones. His nearside goals were always clearly defined. He had to train this much, run that much, fight that match and win. His future goals had had to do with winning international competitions and, if he'd kept up his form, a chance at the Olympics in 92. But fulfilling future goals, he knew, depended on the careful working out of his more immediate ones.

Right now he thought about getting the next drip out and getting rid of another needle, cutting down on the drugs, getting that traction off, sitting up. The future? It was an ideal to think about: to get back to normal, or to find that something good could come out of all this.

It was funny, but those six weeks flew by like an express train. It seemed no time at all until a nurse came up and said, 'I think it's time to hear what you have to say. I'll leave the cuff down and deflate it for a minute.'

That first ventilator and tube Owen was given to assist his breathing was a plastic device with an inflatable cuff which stopped any air from escaping from the tube into the throat, thus bypassing the vocal chords altogether. But the plastic cuff could be inflated and deflated externally by means of a small syringe.

He was so surprised that he didn't know what to say! After six weeks of silence all he could think of was: ''Allo! How's it going, then?'

'Oh,' the Lancashire nurse frowned in disappointment. 'I thought you'd have a posh voice!'

'Some nerve you've got!' he rejoined in his rich Berkshire voice. 'I speak the Queen's English!'

Cathy Walker hurried along the corridor towards Owen's room. She had on a big tweed grandad's coat that flapped around her as she walked. It was becoming something of a trademark.

She walked into his room and into a surprise. 'Hey, Big Ears!' Owen shouted in greeting.

Her heart gave a walloping thump at the sound. The old Owen was alive and well! And there he was, impishly grinning at her from a seated position in a wheelchair. She steeled herself against the tears and joked back at him.

Sybil was there, cheery as always. 'Doesn't he look better now?' she asked.

'Fantastic!' Cathy said. The sound of his low, gravelly voice was like music. 'But now I have to endure more of his insulting remarks!'

One of Owen's early visitors was Jim Mealing from the Southport Judo Club. A few years older than Owen he didn't know him personally but heard of the accident in judo circles. Dark-haired, broad-shouldered Jim came into the room and silently stood by his bedside. In the early weeks that was all he could do. When Owen could talk, a two-way conversation was possible. Jim brought in photos of his two mastiffs. He took over the job of shaving Owen. He straightened Owen's curled fingers, stretching his hands to keep the joints supple. And they talked judo.

The Ogdens, Derek and Dot, came twice a week, Derek chattering non-stop in his incomprehensible Lancashire accent. He had a look on his face, Owen thought, as if he were permanently on the brink of some mischief. When Owen's voice returned, the friendship blossomed. Owen found this stocky, balding man, his father's age, as crazy as his Reading mates had ever been. 'I'll talk dead posh to you,' Derek would say, 'so's you can understand me.'

Owen was amused that he suddenly had a new mate with so little hair and promptly dubbed Derek 'Chrome Dome'. When he saw a photo of the Ogdens taken at a recent wedding with Derek ramrod straight in a new and shiny grey suit, Owen declared he looked like the Tin Man in the *Wizard of Oz*. And on his next visit, Derek marched into the room in his shiny grey suit, playing the part to perfection.

Chapter 9

The Lowery family had established a workable plan to visit Owen each weekend. Sybil took Fridays off from her secretarial job at Reading University and drove up to spend an extra day visiting her son. On Friday evenings, Dave and Adam joined her. At first they spent several weeks in rooms set aside for that purpose within Southport Promenade Hospital. After a while, when they realised that this was going to be a long-term convalescence, they knew they'd not always have access to the rooms which would be needed by other patients' families.

About this time, a Liverpool couple by the name of George and Jean Edwards came into the picture. George had known of Owen for six years when, as the Wigan Judo Club coach, he had travelled to the Junior Nationals at Crystal Palace. He had watched the young lad from Reading play and win.

George Edwards was one of the first to see Owen lying on the mat after he was injured. He only had time to give Dave Lowery his phone number as the distressed father rushed off to follow the ambulance to the hospital. Later, George went to St Helen's

Hospital, then Whiston, and finally found the family at Southport Promenade where Owen had been taken on the second day.

George and Jean reasoned that there wasn't anything they could do for Owen, but perhaps they could do something for his parents. So many a day they would come with bags of sandwiches and flasks of coffee for Sybil and Dave and then sit in the hospital dayroom and wait for the couple to come in for a break and a rest. Over the months the two couples came to value each other's friendship.

In time, George would say to the Lowerys: 'How about coming back to the house for a meal?' At first George picked Sybil up on a Thursday because that was the evening she was alone. He took her back to the house in Billinge and Jean gave her one of her home-cooked meals that made guests want to come back again and again.

Then it became routine for Sybil, Dave and Adam to come along on a Saturday night. And then more often than not they were asked to come over on a Sunday.

'Look, this is daft, you coming and going like this,' Jean said one evening after a meal. She was well used to cooking for her own family, hungry grown-up sons, a mother-in-law who lived nearby, many friends and now the regular guests, the three Lowerys. Someone always seemed to appear on the doorstep. Jean took it all in her stride.

'I think you might as well stay here,' she decided. 'We have two extra bedrooms, so we'll just keep them ready for you at the weekends. George wants you to stay, don't you, George?' And of course George

readily agreed. What Jean didn't say was that there
was a small matter of her son Gary who normally
resided in one of those rooms but who would volunteer
(when she suggested it) to sleep on the sofa downstairs
whenever the Lowerys came.

'We want you to make this your home,' George and
Jean said, and they left the Lowerys no choice but to
agree.

Cathy Walker's visits sometimes coincided with those
of the Ogdens. She'd sweep in, cute as a button,
wearing her outsized coat of dubious vintage. It didn't
take Derek long to tease her about her 'tramp's coat'.

One chilly day Cathy arrived minus the familiar
garment.

'Wer's th' tramp's coat?' Derek asked at once.

'It's disappeared,' she complained. 'I left it in a
friend's car and . . .'

'Hooray!' Derek cheered.

'But my brother gave it to me,' she said. 'It meant a
lot to me!'

'And wer' did he get it?' Derek snickered.

'At a jumble sale . . .'

'I thought so!' he laughed.

But like an old and faithful mongrel, the coat found
its owner again. They both came to see Owen some
weeks later, and in the midst of the visit Derek reappeared. He saw Cathy and the coat, and groaned.
'Look,' he suggested, 'could I buy th' coat? I'll give
you 10p for it!'

Bruce Carr was the lad from Kendal whose own
accident had prompted the charity match in St

Helen's that Sunday in September. Six weeks after his leg had been amputated Bruce had had an artificial limb fitted, and had walked out of hospital with the aid of crutches. Before long he was back at the Kendal Judo Centre relearning judo techniques. Within a year he climbed 'The Calf' – one of the highest fells in the Lake District.

Bruce visited Owen at Southport early in December, along with other members of the Centre. The lads caused quite a commotion at first. A nurse hurried into Owen's room exclaiming: 'There's a crowd of ruffians bearing down on us in the hall. Some of them are pushing others in wheelchairs, but they keep getting out and shoving others in them. It's not any of your lot, is it?'

'Sounds like you could be right,' Owen grinned. And at that point they burst through the doorway.

'Sorry; only two at a time.' The petite nurse pulled herself up to block their way.

The broad-shouldered lads looked down at her and laughed. 'You and who else are going to shift us?'

She decided to withdraw gracefully.

Gary Edwards, George's son, was one of the first to greet Owen. Then Bruce Carr came up and they talked and joked. One by one they came forward and had a word with him, recalling the week he had spent at the Centre only months earlier, climbing the mountains, training with them, running, playing judo. There was a lot of good-natured name calling, back and forth, and a lot of commotion that caused a few nurses some anxiety. Before they left, they made Owen promise he'd come up to Kendal in the summer.

After they left the room, the boys were hushed and solemn-faced. Sybil followed them into the hall and thanked them for coming. They were all devastated to see Owen like that. They'd put on a brave face in front of him, but now, outside, they expressed their shock to each other.

Gary Edwards remembered travelling to France with him for a competition, and sharing a room at the Centre. One was as daft as the other; what times they'd had! Now, Gary didn't know what to say.

Bruce Carr commented to one of the others: 'And I thought I was hard done by! Compared to him, I'm lucky!'

The lads filed out of the hospital in a quieter mood than when they had come in.

Nigel Donahue stopped by for a chat. Nigel was Owen's partner during the match in which Owen fell, and although there had been no body contact between them in that final moment, Nigel may have felt anxious because he was paired with him then. He came quietly into the room, following his father, John.

John Donahue, a regular visitor, came to massage Owen's arms with his special linament. He and Owen were always clowning around, with a lot to say to each other. Today, with Nigel standing there silently, Owen sensed he was shy, so he kept the conversation going himself.

Later, Owen mentioned the visit to Sybil and seemed amused at Nigel's reactions. She explained later to a friend: 'Owen had already adjusted in his own mind to what had happened. He wasn't uncomfortable with it and didn't see why others should be.'

Chapter 10

The hospital Christmas party was planned for a weekday night, so Sybil and Dave couldn't be there. But since it was Owen's first 'public appearance' in a wheelchair, the Ogdens and Donahues said they'd be glad to come in their place.

The party was in full swing, with music even louder than usual, streamers and decorations everywhere, and drinks flowing. Billy Howarth, Owen's hilarious room-mate, was already well underway in that department. Billy was an indefatigable character who, although paralysed from the shoulders down, operated his chair by means of a chin control device. He was dangerous enough manoeuvring that chair when sober. During the festive season, he was definitely a man to watch.

Owen was wheeled out into the hallway, his chair now fitted with a portable respirator for mobility. As they sat in a circle, Owen told Derek about the time John Donahue had tried to kill him.

'When was that, Owen?' Derek asked, dead serious for once.

'When he brought Daisy to me,' Owen said.

John began sputtering, but Owen remained straight-faced. 'There was this cow,' Owen said. 'John took delivery of part of a cow and thought he'd give me a treat.'

'I gave him the best steak,' John explained. 'I thought he deserved it after this hospital food.'

'I asked him for it rare. Rare!' Owen said. 'It was petrified!'

'Maybe she got frightened . . .' Derek offered.

'It was the microwave,' John insisted. 'The nurse must have kept it in too long.'

'I almost choked to death,' Owen accused him.

'I hope you gave Daisy a decent burial,' Derek said, amid laughter.

Suddenly the others noticed Owen trying to say something. He had an urgent look on his face and finally whispered something about 'breathing'.

'He can't breathe!'

'Get a nurse!'

The two wives whipped into action and rushed off to find a nurse. Derek panicked and raced out into the courtyard, then in again, then ran up and down the corridor. A nurse appeared holding her handbag which she stuck on John's rigid arm. He was as still as a statue, too shocked to move.

The respirator's batteries had failed. The nurse quickly 'bagged' Owen with a bellows-type mask, and oxygen was applied until the respirator's batteries were replaced.

The wives returned to the scene to see their men in a right state: one running in circles, the other stiff with fright, clutching a handbag. 'I think they need medical attention themselves,' Dot said to Jean.

A few days later the nurses prepared Owen for his first outdoor excursion. Cathy had arrived for a few days' holiday, and was to accompany the family on a brief shopping expedition.

Owen was a bit nervous while waiting for his parents' arrival and felt rather as if he were about to fight someone good on the mat. But he knew that once they started out, that too would be like a match: OK once you get into it.

He was bundled up to the ears, but even so, the first heady rush of cold was a shock. It had been three months since he had felt fresh air on his face. It may have been a grey, overcast afternoon, but there was a brightness and clarity all around him, more rich and clear than the neon-lighted yellowness of wards and halls. The fresh air made him breathless.

As the group approached Lord Street, people were rushing every which way and the lights of the shops, and the Christmas lights strung across the road and in the trees, dazzled. He hadn't seen Lord Street from this vantage point before, and he was impressed with the grand architecture of buildings set well back on tree-lined plazas. He'd only rushed through the town centre in a car once or twice before and had noticed nothing.

The group turned into Debenhams and its dizzying array of goods. Owen wanted to purchase Christmas presents for the family, but the display was so overpowering, it was difficult to know where to begin.

The chair became stuck in pedestrian traffic past aisles of perfume and jewellery. It got bogged down again in men's wear. Cathy and Sybil held up various shirts which Owen rejected. He finally found one to suit Adam. That was one present down.

He began to get very tired. The music and lights became din and confusion. Other presents were bought hastily and he was ready to return to the hospital.

On the journey back, the wind was cold and miserable, with traces of rain in the clammy breeze. He eagerly returned to the peace and comfort of his room.

When he was a boy, Christmases were spent in Liverpool. First there was a religious service in school to mark the end of term and the beginning of holidays. Everyone sang heartily, thinking of going home. They sang songs about baby Jesus, a manger and angels on high.

> O holy child of Bethlehem
> Descend on us we pray
> Cast out our sin and enter in
> Be born in us today.

Incomprehensible words! The real Christmas was a bearded Santa bringing gifts, family get-togethers and special treats to eat. There was the drive up the motorway, then the arrival at Grandma's house. She had a crucifix on the lounge wall and a picture of Jesus surrounded by angels in the bedroom he and Adam shared. Owen knew who Jesus was: he was a sort of Father Christmas.

Tom Bracewell, another room-mate in the Unit, was a land agent and farmer from Much Hoole who had fallen from a horse in November and was paraplegic. He had kindly lent one of his houses to Dave and Sybil for a few weeks before they had moved into the Edwards' home for their long weekend visits.

New Year's Eve 1987 went out in style. Tom supplied champagne for the four residents of the Intensive Care Ward. Billy was pleased to forego his rum for the occasion. And they all toasted the New Year, wishing each other better luck in the year to come.

Chapter 11

Early in the New Year Cathy decided to take a week's holiday from her job in Stoke, and spend it with Owen. She had only weeks left before leaving for Israel. Although she had been writing to him regularly (and Sybil faithfully answered every letter), she felt the need to be with him personally, to have a serious talk about life and hopefully make a contribution that would be of help to him now, when he needed it most. Who knows what could happen to him (or her, for that matter) in the next few months? She felt it was vital that she use this chance to get through to him about her faith.

Of course they'd had all sorts of discussions over the past year. She thought of them as the train approached Southport. But mostly they had been jokes, mere verbal punch-ups. She was dead serious, but she hadn't a clue how he felt. Really deep down. Did anyone know what Owen thought about anything?

The closer she got to the Southport Hospital the more determined she was to bring it out into the open. Life itself was a grim contest, far more important than a judo title.

They spent hours together in the gymnasium. Physios were now working in earnest to regain some sort of life in his shoulder muscles. Owen's wheelchair was positioned beneath a metal cage with his arms in slings attached to the springs of the cage. The object of the exercises was to get him to shrug his shoulders backwards, to make his arms swing out from his chest. It was a tiring process for him, but he never flinched. It was as if it were just another part of his training programme.

By the end of the week, Cathy was used to the sight of wheelchairs and physio cages, respirators and trachea tubes. She recoiled from them at first, reminders of past horrors and future limitations. As the days passed, she saw that the hospital and all within was simply another part of the world she lived in. And wheelchair-bound youths were going about the business of living just as she was.

They laughed about school, about mutual friends, teachers they had hated, parties they had enjoyed. She read *Middlemarch* to him. They argued about politics, although they were in total agreement about CND, a movement close to both their hearts.

'I've never forgiven you for voting Tory,' he reminded her sternly.

'It was only that once,' she pleaded, cowering. 'I promise never to do it again.'

They discussed homosexuality. Owen said it was probably determined by one's genes or environmental conditions.

Cathy didn't agree. 'It's an age-old problem,' she said. 'Thousands of years ago it was widespread in Sodom. Lot's family was told to leave the city as God condemned the practice and planned to destroy the offenders.'

'Such a long time ago!' Owen laughed. 'How can you base modern values on that?'

'In the New Testament it speaks against it too,' she said shyly. 'That's a good deal more recent. The Scriptures say that it's not the way God created us.'

Owen reminded her that he didn't accept the Bible as a valid authority and then lapsed into one of his jokey moods, effectively ending conversation on the subject.

Times alone were few. Owen's friends filed in and out every day, and evenings were the busiest of all. Owen held court from his wheelchair. There were always half a dozen friends around him and at weekends his family too.

Mornings were quieter. Cathy was asked to leave the room when the nurses washed him, when doctors looked in or when they had to see to his trachea tube. But visitors weren't normally permitted in the mornings, so she was lucky to be allowed in at that time.

The final morning before she left she spoke of Israel. 'It will be great to see the places where Jesus walked,' she murmured.

'Yeah,' he agreed. 'I had a brilliant time there. We did a lot of sight-seeing before and after the matches. We stayed in the new part of Jerusalem, but went around the Old City as well.'

'I'll be staying in a hostel,' she said at last.

On the way home, she thought of how the week had changed her. She no longer felt sorry for Owen. Neither Owen nor any of the other chaps wanted or needed it. She saw that pity is akin to condescension: looking down on the disabled from a position of superiority. Each patient wanted to get on with life and deserved that chance as much as she did. The wheelchairs, clamps, pulleys and ventilators didn't prevent them from having normal feelings and needs.

Owen might now be lumbered with a very different outer skin, but to pity him, she realised, was to insult him. In some ways this eased the tremendous sadness she felt. Life was going to go on as usual. Owen would see to that. And that gave her new hope somehow.

On the other hand, she bitterly regretted that she had not got through to him. He still needed to be spiritually whole; now more than ever. What a great Christian he'd make, she thought more than once. But beneath that jokey exterior you're a hard man to get through to, Owen Lowery.

Chapter 12

'Hi Owen,' the two broad-shouldered strangers said as they walked into the gymnasium. Owen was strapped into physio equipment, his arms exercised by mechanical means. Everywhere was noise and commotion as nurses and physiotherapists worked in every corner of the room, and other patients were taken through their paces in this busy unit.

'Hello,' Owen smiled up at them.

'We're friends of Jim Mealing. My name's John Patterson and he's Gary Volger,' the fair-haired one explained.

'And we're from a judo club in Liverpool,' Gary said.

'That's great.'

'We heard about your accident months ago,' John said.

'And we've been thinking about you a lot,' Gary added.

'Praying for you,' was what Owen thought he heard.

'Yeah, we've been praying for you,' John echoed.

It was not what he would have expected to come out

of the mouths of two strapping blokes. 'Uh, that's nice,' Owen replied.

The two visitors looked around the room and then at each other questioningly. It didn't seem to be the ideal place to do what they had in mind, but they had come all this way to accomplish their purpose, and there was nothing for it but to go ahead.

'We're Christians, y'see, and we really believe in prayer,' John said. 'I mean, we believe in a God who hears and answers prayer. I don't know whether you've read the Bible much,' he went on, 'or whether you've thought much about Jesus. But what he did back then is a great clue to what he can do today. Y'see, Owen, we really believe he's God's Son, and if he is, he's changeless, always the same. Does any of this make sense?'

At first it seemed to Owen that he looked and sounded like a guy in a hurry. Then Owen realised he was simply excited. He spoke with such conviction that it might have been his old friend Andy Syed standing there, waving his arms about, buzzing with something.

'I hadn't really thought about it like that,' Owen admitted.

'What we mean,' said Gary quietly, 'is that we'd like to pray for you now.'

'Would you mind? Would you think we're completely off the rails?' John grinned his dimply smile and Owen thought there was something about him that looked pretty down-to-earth. There was plenty of muscle under that T-shirt. He looked as if he wouldn't stand for any nonsense. Or believe it, either.

'No,' Owen decided. 'I wouldn't mind.' Real action

Gary Volger and John Patterson on the mat

men, these blokes. As Owen wondered what they'd do next, both of them put their big strong hands gently on his head.

'Jesus,' John prayed, like speaking from one Scouser to another, 'we don't know why this has happened. There's a lot we can't understand. But we believe you came to earth because you love us. We believe you're here now because you love Owen. We believe you want something good for him, and that includes healing him . . .'

Gary added: 'Yeah, dear Lord, just bless Owen, and put new strength into him. In Jesus' name, Amen.'

'Amen,' repeated John.

They smiled down on him. They looked a bit like a religious Morecombe and Wise: John, grinning mischievously, Gary, sober, a man of few words. John drew up some chairs, and Gary began to tell Owen about the judo club where he was instructor. They discussed various clubs familiar to all of them, and then asked about Owen's accident and how he'd been coping in the months since then.

'I'm making some progress,' Owen said. 'I got out of bed just before Christmas. That was some Christmas present!'

'Well, we're going to keep praying for you, Owen,' John said as they got ready to leave. 'We'll pray that God does something really special for you.'

'Thanks,' Owen said. 'I need all the help I can get!'

The crazy thing was, no sooner had those two disappeared around the corner than Owen began to shrug his shoulders as he had been unable to moments earlier. At first it was frightening. Then it seemed totally mysterious. Was it his imagination? Or could this possibly be a miracle?

'I had some very unusual visitors here yesterday,' Owen told his mum that Thursday evening after she had arrived. 'They started praying for me.'

'That was very nice of them,' she said. 'Where were they from?'

'They were from a judo club in Liverpool. Don't ask me what church they belong to. They just called themselves Christians. It seemed a bit strange, but they really had something. And I don't know whether it's my imagination or . . .'

'What is it, Owen?' Sybil asked.

'Look,' he said, and gave his shoulders a big shrug.

Sybil just looked in amazement and her face broke out into an enormous grin. Owen hadn't seen one of those in a long time!

After she had left that evening, he reflected on the handful of Christians he'd met in his life: fun-loving Cathy, a great pal even if she had very definite ideas about Christianity. They had stayed good friends for years, and even now she was writing him silly, outrageous letters that were terrific for his morale. And Andy Syed, his classmate, who was as committed to his sport of table-tennis as Owen was to judo. Andy had tried very hard to persuade him to attend his church. Perhaps if the accident hadn't happened he might have gone that next Sunday.

But Christianity had held no interest for him all these years. He had never seen the need. He and Ashley loved to tease Cathy about it, and he could always make her rise to the bait by saying he was an atheist.

These two men, though, he was beginning to realise, had something very special. They had something within themselves, no doubt about it. Was it possible that this had done something for him too?

They kept coming back. Sometimes Gary Volger came with his wife Jill, and sometimes he came with John. Once, when he was alone, he told Owen about his own life.

'You know John,' he smiled, 'never still for a moment. He's always been so enthusiastic, from the first day he joined the club. But once I thought he had gone too far.'

'When was that, Gary?' Owen asked.

'He started to lean on me about going to his chapel with him. I thought: man, he doesn't know who he's talking to! Me, I didn't believe in God any more. Where was he, anyway, in all the mess in the world? Anyway, John kept bouncing around, cheerful as always, even when I refused to go with him.'

Owen smiled inwardly, remembering Andy Syed. 'It's not really my scene,' Owen had told Andy.

'What changed your mind?' Owen asked.

'I lost my mother,' Gary said. 'It was a really bad time for me, and I guess I was finally willing to try anything for peace of mind. When I went to West Derby Chapel and met everyone there, it wasn't bad at all. It was comforting. And I kept going back.

'Then I began to read the New Testament. You know, the story of Jesus, and what sort of life he led. And how he died. That really came down on me hard. I could feel I wasn't thinking the same way,' Gary said.

'All that was preparing me for a special meeting,' he went on. 'Strangely enough, it was on my birthday last November. A bloke named Dave Ross was speaking. He said, "If Jesus came back now, who would be left?" And he asked if anyone would like to accept the Lord right then and there. That's when I made my choice.'

Owen smiled, not fully understanding.

'Jill and I had been married for over two years,' Gary said. 'We had our problems just like the next couple. I'd been in and out of work and that hadn't helped. But after I accepted Christ, my wife says she began to notice a difference in me.'

'What sort of a difference?' Owen asked.

'I don't know. I didn't try to be any different, but she said she wanted what I had. And she started going to chapel with me. She even asked Brian Woods, a friend of ours, to pray for her hearing: she was deaf in one ear.'

'What happened?' Owen asked, flexing his shoulders beneath the blanket.

'She got healed,' Gary beamed. 'Really! I guess it was the proof she needed, because then she gave her life to Christ too. It's fantastic what it's done for our marriage. You can see how many marriages these days end in divorce. I don't know where we'd have been now if we hadn't put our marriage in God's hands.'

'Do you mean he could do something right now and I'd walk out of here?' Owen asked John Patterson during one of his visits.

'Sure he could!' John laughed. 'He can do anything! I've personally seen people healed before my own eyes.'

'People like me?' Owen persisted.

'Not exactly, but that doesn't mean he can't.'

'But *will* he?' Owen pressed him.

'Look, Owen,' John said, 'I have no doubt that if the Lord wanted you to stand now, you would. But sometimes he takes a while over it. If we could understand his mind or predict his ways, we'd be God, wouldn't we?'

'Uh . . . I guess so.'

'But I'm telling you, mate, that this is real. I wouldn't be so cruel as to tell you a lie to make you feel better temporarily. I know God is going to do something wonderful for you. And I believe it includes healing.'

'But what kind of healing?'

'Well, that's the point, Owen. It's not just physical healing you need. There's spiritual healing. You know our bodies are good for some seventy or eighty years and then that's it, but our souls are eternal. Isn't it more important to have the parts that are going to be around longer healed?'

'So when you talk about healing, you're thinking more about the spiritual side?'

'Not necessarily. You know yourself you had more shoulder movement after that first prayer, right?'

'Yeah.' He jiggled his shoulders again. 'I couldn't do that as well before.'

'So I'm not just talking spiritual healing, Owen. But what I am saying is that you want to think about the spiritual side of life. It's going to last longer than either your body or my body.'

'I'll think about it,' Owen promised.

'But,' John grinned and threw a punch near his face, 'I still believe God wants to heal you both ways!'

He had always thought he lived life to the full. He got his greatest satisfaction out of judo, of course, but his friends, and all they got up to, were a tremendous boost. He never thought of himself as anything but happy.

Why then did he keep coming back to John and Gary and Cathy? And old Andy Syed, buzzing? What was it about them? They were really alive, not merely living. They had something he didn't have.

Oh sure, he was lying here, not functioning as he used to. To the observer, they had everything and he had nothing. But the real Owen was still there all right. That hadn't left. Underneath the skin he was 100% normal. And somehow he had the feeling that he needed what they had, and that if he could get it, it would make him happier than he'd ever been – even happier than in the old days.

Chapter 13

Early in May 1988 John Patterson brought a friend along to meet Owen. He was a short, balding, teddy-bear of a man, with a round, rosy face. With dog-collar intact, he might be mistaken for a benign country vicar presiding over a handful of sleepy village folk. But that day he was casually dressed in a woolly jumper, heightening the teddy-bear image. It seemed an unlikely pairing with lean and muscular John.

'This is Brian Woods, my teacher in the old days,' grinned John. 'Better known as "Bubbles" to the lads at school! He kept me on the straight and narrow.'

'Not likely,' Brian objected, laughing. 'This fellow was a right tartar!'

'You surprise me, John,' Owen teased. 'I got the impression that you were always a saint!'

Brian snorted. 'If ever there was a poor starter, he was it! I used to watch him racing around on the back of a motorcycle with another lad, making a dreadful noise in the streets. I remember one day, when I stood watching the fellow as he was shooting past, it seemed that all of a sudden God said to me, "I want that lad."'

'Would you believe it, within a week I was in his house at one of his meetings?' John laughed.

Brian was teaching maths and RE at West Derby Comprehensive in the early 70s, when something quite unplanned and unexpected began to happen. Brian had been meeting with a few young students in his home, talking about the Bible, telling them about Jesus and praying with them when they had problems. This little group grew as other friends started dropping by for coffee and conversation. Soon the front room of Brian's home was crowded with youths as young as twelve and as old as twenty.

They had one thing in common: they were looking for something more out of life. To be sure there were discos and pubs and films to fill the time, and some soon found more exotic amusements, but sooner or later a lad or a girl got to wondering about the spiritual side of life. What's it all about? Why am I here? Is there something I've missed?

'When I drifted into Brian's house there must have been dozens of kids squeezed into it,' said John. 'I guess by the time I left school and Brian moved, there were up to seventy of us going most weeks.'

'Then I lost track of you for a while,' Brian said. 'I wondered whether you'd packed it all in.'

'Well, I messed about for a while,' John admitted. 'You know, you're free and not answerable to anyone. You think life is going to be one long lark. In the beginning, it's perfect, but by 1984 I was thinking: hey, I've left something behind.'

'I got this phone call out of the blue,' Brian told Owen. 'John was asking me what I thought of someone called Billy Graham. He was coming to Anfield for a meeting and John was ringing to ask me whether he was OK. Of course I said yes.'

'So I went to Anfield, walked out there and told God once and for all that I meant business with him from then on,' John said, like a Scouser defying you to doubt him.

Brian was by then in Rainford, teaching at a school there and giving music lessons at home. He was also a lay preacher, visiting churches and house groups where invited and praying for sick people. Many of them were healed.

Before they left that day, John and Brian said a little prayer with Owen. Afterwards, Brian said, 'I believe God is going to do something to you, Owen. But I think he means to start from the inside and work out.'

Accepting the 'sinner' bit would never be a problem. He knew the sort of person he'd been. He may not have had religious training – he wouldn't have paid attention to it even if he had – but he knew what was right and what was wrong. He knew the times he'd done wrong; yes, sinned. Even when he and his mates had got together and laughed about it the mornings after, that didn't wipe out what he had done.

You only had to look around you to see that there was a lot of sin in the world. But somehow that wasn't the point now. It was his sin that concerned him, and what he was going to do about it.

Brian visited Owen weekly, getting to know the lad and telling him a bit about himself too. They were becoming good friends. During the last weekend in

May, John and Brian returned and found Owen with a girl from Reading and his mother, Sybil.

They were all sitting there with him when Brian said, 'How about if we pray for you now, Owen?'

It came as a surprise to Owen – especially since his friend was there. She had already told Brian that she was an atheist, but now she was saying, 'Can I stay?'

Brian replied, 'So long as you don't interfere.' And the curtains were pulled around the five of them.

Owen had been having extra trouble with his neck that day. It couldn't, of course, support itself, and the special headrest, plus a rolled-up towel tucked in each side, kept him as erect as possible. But he was also troubled by an uncomfortable crick in his neck, and it was making him feel even more off-balance than usual.

Brian felt such compassion for his young friend that he started to pray fervently, as if by his own will he could do something for the lad. He was almost fighting with God to do something. Suddenly he relaxed. It was as if God said, 'When you stop trying, then I'll get started.' Brian obeyed.

'Take away the towel,' Owen said after the 'amen'. John got up and slipped the towel away from behind his neck.

'Take away the headrest,' he said, breaking into a grin.

They fiddled with it and took it away, and looked down at Owen who was beaming with delight. His head was erect and he was moving it this way and that. He began to move his shoulders, more than ever before.

'Oh God . . .' the girl gasped.

'You've said it!' Brian reminded her.

'Right in the middle of your prayer,' Owen couldn't get the words out fast enough, 'I felt a click in my neck, like a bone going back into place.' He kept moving his head from side to side to make sure it wasn't a dream.

In the mornings, the nurses completed their night's work by turning him once more, giving him a partial wash, emptying his bag and taking his temperature. It achieved the purpose of rousing him well before 7 am, but then it meant a long wait until visitors arrived in the early afternoon.

The morning following the prayer he found himself thinking about one of his Sixth Form English essays about Hardy's *Return of the Native*. His teacher had chosen for the essay title: 'The sin of pride leads inevitably to destruction'. He had to analyse the character of Eustacia Vye, and trace the events of her life which led to her death. He showed how her vanity, pride and arrogance ruined her chances of happiness.

'The sin of pride leads inevitably to destruction.' Perhaps that was it. In his judo 'box', completely cut off from the rest of the world, he used to enjoy his isolation. He loved unnerving his opponents with that inscrutable dead-pan face of his. If an opponent approached him in a friendly manner with: 'I hear you beat so-and-so last time,' he'd just look at him, not giving anything away. It was a game and he'd get a quiet pleasure from the lad's expression as he turned away. If he were truthful, he'd have to admit that on the mat he felt better than anyone else, as though they were all inferior.

Pride could take other forms too. He liked to give

advice when friends asked, but he never gave anything of himself away. He'd never share any of his problems or deep thoughts with others. That was something private, something for himself alone. Funny how people could misjudge a body. They could say it was unselfish of him to listen to others' problems and not drag out his own. He was beginning to see there wasn't anything unselfish about it. It was only pride.

He thought of his mates from Reading: Andy, Mole, Dave and Ashley. What would they think if he capitulated? They all thought of him as a convinced atheist. Would they laugh if they knew he was praying? Anyway, wasn't that fear another indication of his pride?

Brian came one Wednesday afternoon and for once they had a quiet hour or two together. 'Mind if I read you something from the Bible?' he asked after they'd talked for a while.

'Go on then,' Owen told him.

'A certain ruler asked [Jesus], "Good teacher what must I do to inherit eternal life?"

"Why do you call me good?" Jesus answered. "No-one is good – except God alone. You know the commandments: 'Do not commit adultery, do not murder, do not steal, do not give false testimony, honour your father and mother.'"

"All these I have kept since I was a boy," he said.

When Jesus heard this, he said to him, "You still lack one thing. Sell everything you have and give to the poor, and you will have treasure in heaven. Then come, follow me."

When he heard this, he became very sad, because he was a man of great wealth. Jesus looked at him and said, "How hard it is for the rich to enter the kingdom of God! Indeed, it is easier for a camel to go through the eye of a needle than for a rich man to enter the kingdom of God" (Luke 18:18–25).'

Owen followed the story with great interest. He'd always felt strongly about the distribution of wealth. Many of his socialist friends – and some teachers – were anti-church, as if social justice and Christianity were irreconcilable. Yet here Jesus was making one of the earliest cases for economic equality. He wasn't so out of touch after all!

'Not that Jesus had it in for the rich,' Brian was saying. 'He had wealthy friends and followers. They were on the right path. So why make such demands on this young man?'

'Perhaps he was too greedy?' Owen asked after a moment's thought.

'Perhaps that was his particular weakness,' Brian suggested.

'You mean he might have given a different answer to someone else?'

'That could be. Jesus saw in the young man's heart what he was holding on to. In his case it was his money.'

It put a different angle on the story, Owen thought. If 'riches' were anything that prevented a person from coming to God, then it wasn't necessarily money that was the danger. It could be achievements, ambition, pride. . . .

'He just had to give it all up,' Brian said. 'The funny

thing is, sometimes God asks us to release something to him and when we're free of it, he puts the balance back into our lives in the shape of good things.'

Owen thought about this a great deal over the coming weeks. And when Brian left him a Bible to read, he asked the nurse to open it to that place in Luke's Gospel. She laid it on top of his plastic rack and slid it over to where he sat. That day he began to read the Bible for himself.

'Hey, what's all this?' Mole teased Owen one weekend. He and Dave had come back again, good old faithful mates, and they looked around Owen's corner collection of cards, posters, sketches and cuttings for new bits of interest. Mole was peering at the Bible on his reading stand.

'You could do worse than read that,' Owen quipped. 'Some pretty good stories in there.'

'Hey, Mole, look at this one,' Dave called out, pointing to a card propped up on Owen's TV. Mole and Dave put their heads together and read. It was a little religious tract about God's footprints walking beside a person's footsteps in ordinary times. But when problems and trials come, there's only one set of footprints there, not two. Where's God then? 'That's when I carry you,' God says.

'You don't believe this, do you?' Dave chided Owen, grinning.

Adam had walked into the room a moment earlier and he stood there, waiting to see what his brother would say.

'Yeah, I do,' Owen said firmly to his old mates.

Chapter 14

Brian went away with his family on a camping holiday. On the campsite, he became friendly with a man named Gordon Dacre, who had served in the Rhodesian Army. As they talked they discovered they were both committed Christians. Gordon had just completed a preaching campaign in Africa and was now briefly visiting the UK.

One night they watched TV together in Brian's caravan. In the midst of the news, Owen's face appeared on the screen as part of a Telethon fund-raising appeal. 'I know that fellow!' Brian exclaimed. 'We've been visiting him and praying for him. He's a great chap!'

Gordon listened with interest as Brian spoke of Owen's sporting achievements and the accident. The story touched him deeply.

Later Gordon told of his experiences of fighting spiritual warfare in Africa. He cited many examples of witchcraft and other spirit activity that destroyed people there. 'I think Britain is facing a spiritual battle too,' he said.

'Why don't you come up to Rainford when you have

a few days free in your schedule?' Brian suggested before they parted. 'You and your family are welcome to stay with us, and perhaps I could arrange for you to speak at some meetings locally.'

They parted, but within a few weeks of Brian's return to Merseyside, sandy-haired Gordon was on his doorstep. And shortly thereafter, the two men headed for Southport to visit Owen.

Gordon stood quietly on one side as the two friends spoke together. Brian was concerned about Owen; he thought he looked thinner and weaker than when he last visited. As they chatted, Gordon excused himself and went outside.

Gordon left the room to go off and ask God for a word of knowledge. He felt a spiritual oppression there like a wall preventing God from coming in. He stepped out into the small courtyard off the corridor and stood there silently, waiting for God to speak. Not until he had that assurance did he return to the room.

'Could we pray for you now?' Gordon said at last. Owen agreed and they drew the curtains. But Gordon's commanding voice must have struck terror in the hearts of others in the room. He didn't merely call upon God. He commanded Satan to get away from Owen, and to take those spirits that were binding him and leave.

It may have seemed unusual to Owen, but it didn't embarrass or frighten him. He was too busy being swept up in the power-charged atmosphere. Within a moment he felt as if he were floating above himself, as if the physical Owen was still in bed and the spiritual Owen – the real one – was above him!

It was the most powerful experience of his life so far.

More was to come, however. For hours after Brian and Gordon had left, Owen felt the influence of that prayer. 'These spirits must leave this man,' Gordon had said. It's true I've been bound, Owen thought to himself. It's as if I've been tied up by something to keep me from believing. And yet well into the night he felt something good was going to happen.

He drifted off, not asleep, but confused, floating, not knowing where he was. He was separating again, the physical from the spiritual. A great wrenching, a great dividing, took place. . . .

When he came to nurses were crowding round him, looking down, even pinching his ears and face. 'Owen!' they said, shocked and frightened.

'What was I saying?'

'You don't know? You don't know what you said?'

He could only recall something coming out like a gush. The nurses told him he'd shouted and screamed obscenities. He could scarcely believe them until he remembered again: 'These spirits must leave this man!'

Owen put his head back and experienced a new sensation. He was free. Whatever had tied him down, whatever had kept him from fully accepting Christ, was gone. And there, alone on his bed that night, he felt the freedom to reach out and touch him. He now knew – not just in his head – that Jesus Christ was alive. He knew that Christ had died for him. He knew that he had come to live within him. He knew that he was born again.

'I don't know what the nurses thought about it all,' Owen told Brian that weekend. 'They must have thought I'd gone berserk.'

'People won't always understand, Owen,' Brian assured him. 'The Bible says the cross is foolishness to those who don't believe.'

'But surely if you try to explain . . .' Owen said.

'We're talking about the flesh versus the spirit here,' Brian told him. 'The physical world versus the spiritual world. Those whose lives are dedicated to the physical have a hard time being convinced that the other world even exists! You know that,' Brian grinned.

'You say people won't believe me. But doesn't the Bible say the Christian is supposed to tell others what happened to him? How does that square up?'

'That's right. John and Gary told you, didn't they? You didn't believe at first. But then you were delivered and free to believe.'

'Does it always happen like that?'

'No – definitely not. Some people get tied up in knots spiritually, for example by getting involved in the occult. But most people are caught up in this physical, material world and just don't bother to think about Christ and why he came.'

'And what do we do to them? Hammer the message home?'

'Not exactly,' Brian chuckled. 'That's where the Holy Spirit comes in. He resides within you now; don't forget that. And he will prompt you to give witness to your faith at the appropriate time. He'll even lead you to people who are – like you were – on the brink of believing.

'But the Holy Spirit is not like a built-in pace-maker,' Brian went on. 'God's Spirit merges with man's spirit and we simply find we have a calm inner direction now. We come to a crossroads where we must make a decision (about relationships, work or whatever) and as we pray and read the Bible we find ourselves saying, "Yes, I think this is the way God wants me to go."'

'Then it's not hearing voices?'

'Good gracious, no! God gives us guidance by moulding our conscience and convictions. We say, "God told me to do that," but it's generally a silent "voice".'

'But some people have heard from God audibly, haven't they?'

'In ancient times, yes, before the Scriptures were readily available. Sometimes today, too, in remote areas where there's no other way for God to get through. But normally, in our situation, we can expect the Holy Spirit to comfort, direct and strengthen us in a strong internal way. Here, read this . . .' and Brian turned to the book of Hebrews, chapter 1, and laid it on Owen's lap.

'In the past God spoke to our forefathers through the prophets at many times and in various ways, but in these last days he has spoken to us by his Son,' Owen read.

'The best way of hearing God's voice today, Owen, is by reading his words. It's funny, people may have turned away from God in recent times, but the Bible is still the world's bestseller.'

The next time Cathy visited Owen it was like a family reunion. There were no barriers. For the first time in their long friendship, there was nothing to hold back.

They compared notes on books they read. They discovered they were both reading C. S. Lewis. Cathy was going through *Mere Christianity* again; Owen was enjoying the *Screwtape Letters*.

Finally she pulled the curtain around them and they prayed together. Cathy felt so full of gratitude that the words came tumbling out easily. But then Owen began to pray and she could only shake her head in amazement. A miracle!

When she opened the curtain, they found two nurses grinning. 'You've been a long time! What's been going on in there?'

Before she left, Owen confessed: 'I used to like to hear you talk about your faith at school.'

Cathy looked at him in surprise. 'But I thought I was boring you! You didn't believe it, and I didn't want to force you . . . or push it . . .'

Owen said, 'You weren't boring me. I always enjoyed hearing about it.'

On his next visit, Brian asked a nurse for a piece of bread. He poured some Ribena into a glass and, after the curtains were closed, gave Owen his first Communion.

'Christ gave up the rights to his own body,' Brian said. 'He chose to make that sacrifice so that we could enter into fellowship with our Creator.

> There was no other good enough
> to pay the price of sin

He only could unlock the gate of heav'n
and let us in

We are not good enough, and there are no works that can make us good enough. But faith in Jesus Christ makes us acceptable to God. That's why we're here now.

'Take this bread to remember his body broken for you.' Brian put the bread into Owen's mouth.

'Take this cup to remember his blood shed for you.' And he held the glass to Owen's lips.

At Maiden Erlegh school, when Owen had been in the Sixth Form, everyone knew the names Lowery and Syed. The two Lowery boys, Owen and Adam, won judo matches and awards regularly, and the two Syed boys, Andy and his younger brother Matthew, were making much the same impact in their sport of table-tennis.

One day in June Sybil was outside the school on Silverdale Road waiting to pick up Adam. Mrs Syed came over to the car and looked in at Sybil. 'How was he last weekend?'

'Much the same, thanks,' Sybil smiled. Mrs Syed always showed such concern; she never failed to ask about Owen when they met.

'Andy would love to go up and see Owen,' Mrs Syed said.

'He'd always be welcome,' Sybil said. 'In fact, we'd be glad to give him a lift up any weekend.'

Mrs Syed looked worried. 'That's good of you, but I think we'd have to bring him ourselves. He might not be well enough . . .'

'What's wrong?'

'We're not sure what it is, but sometimes he can hardly move.'

'I met Mrs Syed a few days ago,' Sybil told Owen that weekend in Southport, 'and she said that Andy's not in good health.'

'Still?' Owen was surprised. 'He told me he was having muscular trouble the night before my accident. He'd been unable to play for months, and it was getting him down then. What's the problem?'

'Doctors don't seem to know what it is. Many days he can't even drag himself out of bed.'

'That's rough,' Owen said, and after his mother had left for the night he cast his mind back to that evening at Andy's house, to their lofty thoughts and serious conversation about sport and life and death. Now they were both having to do more than just talk about it.

Not long afterwards Owen received a letter from Andy:

. . . some specialists suggest ME, but tests are still being made. It's almost unbelievable – in fact 'I know not in the whole range of language terms sufficiently expressive to describe my infernal condition' to quote from an 'O' level author!

However, it's *good* to hear that some improvement has taken place for you, and even better to find out (through Cathy Walker) that you have become a Christian. I know this relationship with the living God must be helping you through what must be the toughest test of your life.

I hear that you have remained your cheerful outgoing self, but it must be tough. I must admit that I have found it hard to cope with the sudden loss of what I now know to be the false security which society, in general, values so highly. But I believe the answer is for our security to come from the knowledge that God loves us and that our names are written in heaven.

With you in something of a similar position to me, I think about you much and I hope and pray that you will hang in there and come through what must be one of the hardest tests life can possibly bring upon someone. In fact, it's almost impossible fully to recognise and appreciate the extent of the predicament you are faced with. But God knows it, and I'm sure he'll be with you every step of the way.

Ever your Christian friend,

Andy Syed

Chapter 15

Carol Porter, a pretty blue-eyed student with blonde curly hair, arrived at Southport Promenade on a Southport College placement assignment two days after Owen's accident. On her first morning in the Spinal Injuries Unit, she took in the vast units of machinery surrounding the beds. The patients looked quite small and insignificant compared to the technology that enveloped them.

Her eyes fell on one sleeping figure. The machinery was heaving and sighing all about him. She glanced at the chart at the foot of his bed: OWEN LOWERY AGE 18.

'Can you come here, please?' a nurse called for help. Carol was ushered into a cubicle enclosed by a curtain and suddenly everything made her feel claustrophobic. She fainted.

'There was a bit about him in the paper,' Mrs Porter said later on in the week as the family were having a meal. 'Pity you missed him.'

'Missed who?' Carol asked.

'Owen Lowery. You know, the lad hurt at judo. He's at the Promenade.'

'I saw him,' Carol said. 'I work in his unit.'

She worked most Wednesdays in nearby rooms, but occasionally she was asked to assist the physios in the Intensive Care Unit and sometimes she helped with Owen. Her placement ended before Christmas and after that other work and study kept her busy elsewhere.

The following June Carol heard about the 'Judo Throw' event organised for Owen by Jim Mealing from Southport and Steve MacDonald of Neston. They planned a judo demonstration along the Promenade that would begin at the south end and continue one mile to the north end. Twenty judo members would be involved in the actual contests, though parents and friends would provide the essential back-up for moving mats, organising collections and driving cars. Jim Mealing asked Carol if she'd help with a bucket to collect gifts from passers-by.

It was a cold, grey, blustery day with the promise of rain. A poor start for an event that needed plenty of spectators standing around. Lads from various judo clubs began to appear by 11 am. Jim Mealing's mastiff Zep came dressed in a judo suit and was the star attraction of the day. For an hour, the time it took for the members to throw each other from one end of the Promenade to the other, the heavens opened. Lads performed on wet mats with wind and rain throwing them as much as their opponents. A fraction of the expected crowd turned up, and those who did soon ran for cover. Even so, more than £1,000 was collected, which included amounts donated through sponsorships. Jim and Steve could only speculate how much they'd have collected in fair weather. They were all determined to come back and have another go later on.

After the event Carol was invited to join the group for a drink at the Windmill where they went to escape the rain. She stood near Owen, doubting that he'd know who she was.

'You remember Carol?' Matron pointed her out to Owen.

They said their hellos, but he was busy chatting with his friends. Before she left, he said, 'Come and see me.' And then he added, laughing, 'I'm not going anywhere!'

Carol was shopping in Lord Street a week later, having just bought a bouquet of flowers for her mother, when she bumped into Jim Mealing who was on his way to the hospital. 'Why don't you come with me?' he suggested. 'I'm going to visit Owen.'

Clutching her flowers, she went back with Jim to the familiar ward and entered Owen's room.

'For me?' he feigned surprise. 'You shouldn't have!'

She blushed and murmured that they were for her mother. He laughed and the ice was broken. After that she began dropping in every week.

One Thursday evening Sybil arrived at the unit and laid some architect's drawings across Owen's knees.

'What's all this, Mum?' he asked.

'I was talking to an occupational therapist in Wokingham,' she said. 'She advised us to make certain changes to the house for when you come home. So I took our house plans along to an architect several weeks ago. I got these back yesterday.'

Their large 1950s semi-detached house on Falstaff Avenue wasn't designed for wheelchair living, but the architect had sketched out an extension to the ground floor which could be a flat for Owen. For a long time he studied the familiar shapes of the rooms he'd known since childhood. It looked like a skeleton of a house put down like that. Until nine months earlier it had been home.

'I'd rather stay here,' he said finally.

'Here? In the hospital?' She didn't understand.

'No, in the North. Somewhere around Southport, where our friends are now.'

It took her completely by surprise, but when she thought of nearby friends made since the accident, and old friends here who had become closer still, she realised she should have been prepared. George and Jean Edwards for a start: they had opened their home every weekend without fail for nine months. And Derek and Dot Ogden who were such a tonic for Owen; and the Donahues who brought gifts and organised raffles and visited every week. There were new friends for Owen too – David and Lisa Riding, John and other Christian friends. Each one was more than an acquaintance; they were all close friends.

However, there was Adam to consider too. He had another year of his 'A' levels to complete so nothing could be considered until he had finished those. Would he want to leave Reading and his friends there?

Sybil had already looked ahead to the time when Owen would be discharged. She knew she'd have to resign from her job. In that case, did it matter so much where she lived? The only question remaining concerned her elderly parents: would they stay in Reading with no one left?

Suddenly it all seemed overwhelming. How would they know what was best?

Chapter 16

One Saturday in August the Lowery family had their long-promised day's outing to the Kendal Judo Centre. The hospital van was booked, the nurses washed and dressed Owen early, and he was already in his chair by the time Mum, Dad and Adam arrived in his room.

The lads at the Centre had urged Owen to return. Only the year before, just before the Snowdonia trip with Ashley and Cathy, Owen had gone to Kendal and spent a week there. At this unique Centre, lads from all over Britain lived, trained and played judo together and all pitched in to maintain the property.

Recently Tony McConnell, resident coach-manager, had rung Sybil and Dave to make arrangements. 'There's a few steps around here,' he said, 'but the lads will help with his chair.'

The van drove up through picturesque stone-walled lanes and beautiful countryside. Dave turned into the cobbled courtyard. The building and environs looked more like a country inn than a judo centre. Then the lads came out and there were boisterous greetings all round.

This was the first outing of its kind since Owen's accident and only to himself did he admit his anxieties about it. He was concerned about the lads' reaction to him and his chair. He didn't want them to make a big deal of it or be upset. He wouldn't like that. However, if they went on with their training and carried on in an ordinary way it could be a great day for everyone.

The lads rushed forward and watched Dave organise the lift with Owen's chair on it. Then they got to work and many hands grabbed bits of the chair and hoisted it over the rough cobbled yard and into the building.

Owen hadn't remembered all the stairs. Last year he'd run up and down them many times a day. Now lads eagerly manoeuvred the chair round corners, through corridors and up stairs at top speed.

Watching the weight training Owen talked over old competitions with Mark Preston, whom he had defeated in the British Closed Final. They laughed about the time Steve 'Obbalob' Scott found himself in a spot of bother when he drove his motorbike unlicenced, uninsured and untaxed.

Owen recalled his earlier visit to the Centre, and what good training it offered. He remembered the special mountain circuit (better known as the 'Barney Rubble Circuit') where he and other lads had run up the side of a mountain doing exercises with lumps of rock for weights, and how their coach had told them off if they picked small rocks to carry.

It was customary to go into judo training after lunch, but when he asked Tony McConnell about it, he said they would be doing circuit training instead.

'Why is that, Tony?' Owen asked.

At first Tony looked embarrassed. 'We thought it would upset you.'

Owen grinned up at him. 'It wouldn't upset me. I was quite looking forward to it.'

'Right then,' Tony said. 'When you come again we'll do judo for you!'

Later Owen and family joined the lads for tea. His mates Gary and Mark sat on either side of Owen and took turns feeding him. Then other lads joined in by feeding Gary and Mark. Soon it began to resemble an assembly line. 'We were all quite relaxed and had good fun,' Owen said.

One of the lads explained later why everyone took it in their stride. 'We were used to dealing with such problems when Bruce Carr was injured. When he came back to the Centre after his accident, we had to get used to seeing him struggle to get sorted out again. I guess we learned how to handle the situation and think about how the other fellow feels. He doesn't want to be made a fuss of or treated like a baby. He just wants to be normal like everyone else.'

Owen was asked if it had bothered him at all to remember his former visit. 'No,' he shrugged. 'I felt the same as the last time. I didn't feel any different. They seemed pleased to see me and I had a great time.'

John Webster has been a rehabilitation helper at Southport for nine years. His swarthy, smiling face was an encouragement to Owen from the first month. John was always glad to help make him comfortable, feed him or just sit and chat for a few moments.

After observing Owen in the Spinal Injuries Unit,

he felt he knew him as well as anybody. 'I've seen Owen when he's been very poorly,' John told a hospital visitor one day, 'and even then he's been more interested in others than in himself! If you ask him how he's feeling, you'll not get more out of him than, "Not too bad, thanks, John." He's a real genuine bloke. In fact, one of the most thoughtful and giving lads you could meet.

'I've watched some videos with him, videos of him playing judo. He sat there, analysing the holds and falls quite matter-of-factly, saying, "I could have done better there," or, "I shouldn't have done that one!" But there was no trace of pity or regret.

'Did you know he visits a cancer patient every Saturday in another hospital? That's the way he is: always thinking of others. I'm not a religious man, but with Owen I'd say whatever's been taken away, something else has been given back.'

Owen's Saturday visits were to Tom Wright, a patient in Liverpool who was transferred to Southport during the summer of 88. He was in the big 'G' Ward near the Intensive Care Unit. Forty-year-old Tom had been a boxer known as 'Tom the Bomb', but a degenerative disease first left him walking with sticks and eventually confined to a wheelchair. He had an operation on his neck, but even so things went from bad to worse.

During his months in Southport, Tom and Owen struck up a special friendship as only two tough fighters can, and enjoyed chatting together. Tom was transferred in the autumn and for some months Owen lost touch. The following year he found out that Tom was at St Joseph's Hospice, Ince Bundell, seriously ill with cancer of the spine. Owen asked his parents to take him to visit Tom in the hospital mini-bus.

A new weekend routine started for the Lowery family and each Saturday, with Carol, they visited the 'Jospice' (as it is locally known). As the months passed, Tom's condition required that he lie in a hammock above his bed. On the wall at eye level hung three of Owen's poems, telling of his quest and how he found the light of God at the end of his tunnel.

Chapter 17

Early in 1988 Owen was approached by staff from Granada Television to appear in ITV's Telethon, the twenty-four-hour charity appeal that centres on a variety of needs throughout the UK. The aim was to cite a particular patient in the Southport Spinal Injuries Unit, do a feature on him, and encourage viewers to support the Telethon using him as an example.

Though Owen was at first reluctant to be filmed for national viewing, to be seen being lifted, carried and exercised, he agreed and the camera crew arrived at Southport, taking a full day to film his brief segment.

The programme was aired in June 1988 and caused much interest. An old video showed him on the mat, rushing forward for a throw, then accepting a medal on a podium. Next there were photographs of a young strong body, a smiling youth and his collection of awards. Finally the camera moved to the present, to a fragile, limp body being carried by nurses from bed to chair, attached to the ever-present ventilator. That strong expressive face and cheerful eyes must have challenged the most hardened viewers to run for their chequebooks.

When the segment was released, the focus was entirely on Owen, his need for finance and a specially adapted van, a computer and the other pieces of equipment essential to his rehabilitation. The presenter said, 'We want to help Owen. Won't you help us to do so?'

Owen and his family were delighted that he was able to help such a worthy effort as Telethon. They were also pleased that his segment created such good response. A TV presenter later called Owen a 'cornerstone of the fund-raising effort of Telethon'. £2.3 million was raised in the Northwest alone and approximately £22 million countrywide.

Friends began to ring the Lowerys in Reading or pop into the hospital at Southport. 'We've sent our cheque for Owen,' they would say. 'We've designated it for him.' Others related to them how their own friends were prompted to give to this boy whom they didn't know.

'But it's not going to Owen,' Sybil would say to them. 'It's for the unit. We've known that from the first and that's fine with us.' Many of their friends were surprised and disappointed. They thought they were giving to Owen's Trust Fund. They felt the TV segment had misled them.

'Look, the money will go to others like Owen,' Adam had to remind some who objected. 'That's what's important. There will be trustees who will see to the fair distribution of it.'

Later the family learned of the thorough job done by the trustees in studying the applications that came flooding in for a portion of the Telethon fund. In the end, 1,000 deserving organisations in the Northwest shared the sum that was sent in from the Northwest. Trustees in other parts of the country divided out the money collected in the other regions.

Owen was delighted to learn that he was to be given a £12,000 computer as Telethon's thanks for his efforts. This was the latest model with infra-red signal attached to a sip and puff tube coming from a head-band. He longed to write letters to his friends in Reading, answer the many greetings of well-wishers who had written over the past year and set down some of those poems which were knocking around in his brain. He had some ideas for a short story as well. . . .

Months later, in September 1988, the TV crew returned, having asked Owen to film a sequel in which he thanked people for giving to the Telethon. They brought along a computer and filmed him sitting alongside it, so viewers could see how their money was spent. When the filming was finished, the crew left, taking the computer with them. Someone told him: 'We'll order yours now.' Owen eagerly anticipated his first opportunity of independence since his accident a year earlier. But months passed and he continued to wait.

Owen wasn't the only one waiting. Sybil had written to the British Judo Association shortly after the accident, enquiring as to whether Owen was entitled to any insurance money. The BJA sent a claim form and Sybil filled in one form, the doctor another. Finally word came back: yes it had all been processed and Owen would get the money in one year's time when it was proved that his injury was permanent. The sum mentioned was £2,000.

Twelve months had passed and Sybil wrote again to the BJA; another form completed by Sybil and the doctor was dispatched. And then she again waited.

Owen's Trust Fund was set up by Don Werner, Owen's long-time judo coach in the Reading area. This was kept at Lloyd's Bank, Crowthorne, and in the first year had risen to a total of £10,000. This came from friends, judo colleagues and families through individual donations, small charity matches, raffles and other sponsored events.

Then Owen appeared on TV in the Telethon appeal and donations slowed. Some of those who had contributed earlier thought Owen would be well endowed now, with a nationwide appeal bringing in vast amounts for him and the family. Others thought he'd be set up for life, and there were even those who concluded he had made a fortune out of the appeal! It seemed that now any private attempts to raise further funds for him would be less successful.

Finally Don Werner decided it was time to turn over the Lloyds balance to Sybil so that she could deal with it as they saw fit. The Lowery family had been overwhelmed with Don's efforts, and were continually amazed at the kindness and generosity of those who gave. Owen was touched and humbled by every gift, whatever the size.

They began to discuss what equipment Owen would need. After the computer, the single most important item on the agenda was a van. That would cost well over £10,000, but it was essential for Owen's mobility.

They were also beginning to think more seriously about moving North. Their home in Reading, they knew, might not fetch as much as they'd need for a specially equipped one in the Southport area, but relocation was what Owen wanted and they were content.

Despite a growing list of financial complications, and petrol and telephone bills going through the roof, Sybil remained her unflappable self. 'Somehow things will get sorted out,' she told a friend over a cup of coffee, 'and we won't end up in debt.'

Chapter 18

An experimental operation was recommended as Owen's diaphragm had ceased to function normally. It was suggested that he have an intercostal stimulator implant, in which an electric current passes from a box shaped like a pacemaker fitted under the skin of the chest through the intercostal muscles to help them contract.

Doctors stressed that success was not guaranteed, but that it might make it possible for him to breathe without the ventilator. After discussing it with the family Owen agreed to try this procedure. Hospital staff arranged for him to travel to King's College Hospital, London for the operation.

Owen travelled in the ambulance one morning in November with Dr Watt and Sister Bingley in attendance. The first incident occurred on the motorway when the ambulance ran out of petrol. The driver radioed for help, but that arrived with no petrol. A second call produced not just the petrol but another ambulance.

The journey might have been a scene from a *Carry On* farce. As the ambulance approached London, the

driver radioed ahead for a police escort off the motorway. The police operator asked for the name of the
accompanying doctor.

Driver: 'Watt.'

Police: 'Dr what?'

D: 'Yes.'

P: 'Yes, what?'

D: 'Watt.'

P: 'What?'

D: 'Watt. Doctor Watt!'

P: 'What doctor?'

D: 'Doctor Watt!'

P: 'What is his name?'

D: 'Yes; Watt is his name!'

Finally:'Will you spell his name?'

D: *'Whisky-Alpha-Tango-Tango!'*

P: 'Oh . . .'

After this exchange the driver turned to his
laughing passengers and said, 'These Southerners are
all ignorant anyway.' And Owen, offended, replied in
his best Cockney: 'What d'ya mean, ignorant?'

Back in Southport in time for Christmas celebrations
Owen, despite the recent operation, was feeling
altogether stronger than the previous Christmas,
when the brief half-hour excursion to Debenham's
had left him exhausted. He was glad to be wheeled
down a long stretch of Lord Street, enjoying the lights,
moving in and out of shops, buying gifts for the family.
And a gold butterfly brooch for Carol, with garnets
inlaid.

There were new friends to celebrate with this year.
John Patterson invited the Lowerys and Carol to

dinner at his family home in West Derby, Liverpool. Brian Woods gave them all a Christmas tea at his cottage in Rainford. Previously an organ scholar, Brian entertained the group playing carols on his prize Bechstein Grand and afterwards they all joined in singing around a blazing fire.

Old friends were never far away. There were dinners with George and Jean Edwards at the Lowerys' 'second home'. Other meals and outings filled Owen's calendar. And a very special evening was spent being entertained by George Hamilton IV!

Carol's mum spied a small advert in the paper: George Hamilton IV appearing in concert at the Leyland Road Methodist Church. She showed it to Owen. Could it be the *real* George Hamilton? Apparently it was. Derek Ogden was mad about country music so Owen suggested he might want to come along.

Derek wasn't so sure about the venue. In fact he was very apprehensive. 'What will I do in a blooming church?' he asked, but his love of 'country' bore him on.

It was an extraordinary concert. George Hamilton IV, who had sung at the Grand Ole Opry, on television, in Hollywood and at many famous spots abroad, was this time travelling quietly and simply throughout Britain, singing and speaking in churches that held hundreds rather than auditoriums that held thousands. He had no backing group; he used only his guitar. He wasn't doing this for money or prestige. Just fellowship.

He spoke about the Christmas story, then sang a

carol. He told about Jesus and then sang about why he came. The story of Christ – from manger to cross – was told in song and informal conversation. Just a simple church and modest setting, but a world-famous singer giving everything he could: perhaps a modern example of the Christmas story itself. His audience was captivated.

Afterwards, he went among the people signing tapes of his songs. Derek Ogden wasn't about to miss his chance! Hefty, robust and not easily intimidated, he approached George Hamilton and then suddenly lost his voice. The singer, well over six feet, looked down on this star-struck fellow and, pen in hand, asked, 'Who's it to?'

Derek stared up at him, unable to get the words out.

'Who am I signing it to?'

It was all he could do to say, 'Derek.'

'One "r" or two?'

His wife and friends couldn't stop laughing as he stood there, transfixed.

On the way home, Derek heartily sang a song he'd heard that night:

> Bringing in the sheep
> Bringing in the sheep

He was enjoying himself so much that no one had the heart to tell him it was 'sheaves' that were to be brought in.

Another holiday outing was to Sheffield to hear a university performance of *Godspell*. Dave took the Lowerys and Carol to the Saturday matinee in the hospital van. Adam was glad to go along since he'd played the drums for the Reading Youth Theatre's production of *Godspell* two years earlier.

This time, Cathy Walker was one of the players. In a clear, sweet voice she sang her part. After the show she walked back to the van with them. 'You were the best, Walker!' Owen conceded as they were leaving.

'Wow, and coming from you! Thanks!' she laughed at this rare compliment.

Adam was offended. 'He never went to see me play in *Godspell*,' he told her.

'Now who would want to go and listen to a turnip?' Owen retorted.

Just before Christmas friends in Billinge told Dave and Sybil: 'They're building on an old farm nearby. Why don't you go up there and have a look at the site?'

The Lowerys had been thinking about the Lake District, and had made several trips to Kendal. But the houses available were too isolated and there were no shops in the village.

So one weekend the couple drove through Billinge and up a hill surrounded by farmlands. Neat rows of houses had been built recently to the very edge of neighbouring farms, but a new development was underway that would incorporate an old barn and some stone-built farm cottages.

The builder unrolled his drawings and spread them out on the bonnet of Dave's car. There was a plot at the very end of the cul-de-sac, with windows planned to look up to Billinge Hill, the highest point in Merseyside.

'Owen could have that room,' Sybil pointed to the

one overlooking the hill. It had space for a bathroom en suite.

'And this one across the hall could be for his computer and work area,' added Dave.

They walked off by themselves and talked it over, and felt this could be the one.

Sybil looked in her handbag. 'I've used my last cheque,' she sighed. She knew David never carried a chequebook with him.

He pulled out his wallet and plucked out a crumpled cheque. 'Don't know when I put that there,' he grinned. He wrote out a deposit for £250, and the house was theirs.

On Christmas eve all the noise and revelry, the festive cheer suddenly seemed very abrasive to Owen. He turned aside from the food offered to him and from the conversation of family and friends. It was hardest of all for Sybil and Dave, who couldn't get a word out of him. They sat there chatting with visitors who came, hoping they wouldn't notice how depressed Owen was.

Sybil felt very tired. It wasn't the physical strain of driving back and forth, holding down her job four days a week and staying with him at weekends. It was the emotional strain of seeing him so discouraged, and being unable to do anything. Perhaps he was disappointed about the operation. They had all tried to avoid pinning their hopes on it. The electric current had caused such discomfort for him that it distressed her to see him with one more worry. When the doctors concluded that it had not been successful they were all inclined to think it had all been for nothing.

She wondered if he were wishing he wasn't there. They never discussed it, but how was she to know what he was thinking? He could be thinking that now.

She thought of all the efforts made by doctors and nurses to save him in the early days. Was it such a good idea to keep a person alive like that? She wasn't so sure. Anyway, the doctors didn't give you a choice. It wasn't a question of asking the patient or his family. The decision had been made for her. To the doctors it was a question of ethics.

In many countries, she learned, there were no quadriplegics. The equipment to save the severely disabled simply wasn't available.

Anyway, she thought dispiritedly, it's such an emotional decision. If you were given the chance to save someone you loved, who wouldn't say 'yes'?

She looked over at Owen again. Despite his current depression, she was sure he would want to be saved. He had always clung to life.

On Christmas morning Brian arrived while Owen was still in bed, and drew the curtain round the two of them. They prayed together and then Brian gave Owen Communion. As Brian pulled back the curtains, Sybil walked into the room and Owen was smiling broadly. She could see the cloud had lifted. 'I'm OK now, Mum,' he said.

Chapter 19

Owen's corner of the Intensive Care Ward was getting more crowded by the minute. Now along with bed, respirator, wheelchair, cabinet, TV and other equipment, the computer and all its accessories became the focus of activity and interest.

His Telethon thank-you gift finally arrived in February 1989. It was an Apple MacIntosh II, and the computer screen contained an image of a typewriter keyboard. Soon Owen went from chasing the cursor around the keyboard at three words per minute to fifteen words per minute.

'Put on my headpiece, will you, John?' he'd say to the passing attendant. Months before, his headphones tuned him into the outside world of pop music, a welcome relief from the sounds of other TVs, cassettes and general hospital commotion. Now his headpiece, with the attached mouth tube, provided more than passive entertainment. He could now communicate on paper – like anyone else.

It meant he could type directly to friends and not depend on his mother to do the secretarial chores. And when several classes of schoolchildren began to write to him, there weren't enough hours in the day to keep up with replies to everyone.

His first letter, however, was to his mother:

> Hi Mum; how's it going? This is harder work than I thought! I don't fancy this secretary lark much! At least there's no telephone to answer yet. It's a good job young Ms Porter's here to help find some of the letters and keep up my Ribena levels or I'd be in a right mess. I've got the hang of the printer now so you've had it once and for all.

Sybil was kept busy filing the letters Owen received or wrote while in hospital.

> Dear Owen,
> I am sorry to hear about your accident and I hope that you will carry on getting better. A couple of months ago my dad fell out of the loft and broke his wrist, a vertebra and a bone beneath his shoulder. The night that he did it, I slept next door and played with their cats.
>
> Daddy has started building a pond. It has two layers of plastic and has lots of gaps in between some bricks. The next door neighbour Trevor brought over some of his pond plants for it and said that we could keep their tadpoles. On Saturday we got five small goldfish from a pet shop in Stroud and a pot of flake fish food that floats. The fish won't eat the tadpoles because their mouths are too small.
>
> Lots of love,
> Sarah Kew, 9 yrs

> Hello Squidge,
> Well if you will call me dopey I feel obliged to keep up the attack. How's old blundering Adam by the way? Insult him for me, will you? Did you know his last message to

me was 'stay slim, ha ha'? The little swine! (He's such a poser, isn't he? I'm surprised he hasn't emigrated to California by now!)

And how's my old buddy getting on? Have you become a silicon whizz-kid yet? And I thought you weren't the scientific type! I shall expect mega-long intellectual epistles courtesy of the chip and a summary of the contents of 'the Observer's Book of Bishops'.

Did I tell you I've been asked to join a band? I waffle on so much that I can't remember. The band consists of a professional drummer, a third-year historian and (wait for it) three sixth-year architects! Not bad, eh, for a little fresher like me? What d'ya mean, 'so what?' Huh! Move over Tracey Chapman! They're nearly as nutty as you are, Owen me old crackpot, but not quite of course.

Here's looking at you kid, me old chum,
    Cathy

Dear Owen,
How are you, you old bolshie? Many apologies for not keeping in touch. Being a student, one picks up bad habits: not writing to friends, becoming drunk given the opportunity, etc. However, by the time you receive this letter, I'll have become a Spritzer-drinking yuppie bearing the indispensable filofax and *Financial Times*.

Hope I can see you before British Rail's special offer expires.
    Take care
    Ashley

Dear Owen,
I am now also officially allowed to drink (which takes the thrill out of it). College is totally boring. I'd rather be training. We're off to Holland tomorrow. I'm dead nervous as I have never fought abroad before. I'm not

quite sure what to expect, as they're supposed to be very strong.

Christmas was OK. Phil and I went out a few times and got paralytic. I resisted loads of beautiful ladies (ha ha) and so did Phil (ha ha) . . .

Cheers,
Jason

Dear Owen,

I am ten in August. My granny and grandad live in Southport. My mum was in the Royal Marsden Hospital but now she is nearly better.

Love from Timothy Ashdown, age 9 yrs

Dear Owen,

Hope you are feeling much better after the accident. Our class knew about the accident from my teacher Miss Bolton's *Renewal* magazine.

The Lord gave me a picture and it was of a man in bed, and in a flash the Lord came and said to the man: 'I am with you always.'

Bye for now,
Deanna Jeffrey, age 8

Dear Owen,

Well, work experience so far has been better than I expected. Among the good bits: sitting in reception all day waiting for someone to acknowledge you. The high-light of my day thus far has been talking to a plant called Arnold. He feels people take him for granted.

One of my colleagues called Simon has just asked me to help set up a badminton court. He then went off to chat up the sauna lady and disappeared for an hour. This I could understand if she wasn't so incredibly ugly.

Yes, this should be interesting 'work experience'. I

figure I work about six minutes in the hour. Hope I can keep up!

Have you spoken to your brother about the Holland competition yet? I was on at the same time as his match, but from what I can gather he had the fight practically won with ten seconds to go, when he made the famous fatal mistake: he relaxed. As I was stepping onto the mat for my semi-final I heard a tremendous cheer which I later found out was Adam being thrown. Well at least 'Magilla Gorilla' has learned something from the trip!

As for me, my first fight was against a Belgian. I started off well enough attacking and driving him to defence, but at 1.10 minutes I lost concentration for a split second and got thrown.

Don threw a fit at me for the rest of the fight for not setting him up properly and going for arm locks instead of strangles. He of course was just defending, but I eventually caught him with *Tai-otoshi* to *Makikomi* . . .

    Cheers,
      Jason

Dear Owen,
My brother used to do judo. When my brother came home he did a judo throw on my other brother. I have three brothers: James, Declan and Edward. James is the one who used to do judo.
    John Wooloughan, age 9
      Rochester, Kent

Dear old pal,
I'm learning all kinds of useful information in my phonetics course: like knowing the difference between an alveolar fricative and a glottal stop. Of course I'm not sure how this helps me to write properly. (This is where you're supposed to say: 'Oh no, Cathy, I think you

express yourself very well,' and I say, 'Oh no, surely not?' and you say, 'Yes really,' and I say, 'Aw shucks!')

I have Spanish Lit at 9 am. What a time to have it, huh? I mean, rotten. Jolly dashed bad show, what? I used to have 'A' level French Lit first thing Mondays at school, and it tended to be a dialogue of philosophical/ religious debating between Mr Sharma and me, whilst the rest of the class slept on, getting increasingly bored with chatterbox Walker . . .

God bless,
Cathy

Dear Owen,
I heard about you when our teacher Miss Packington read about you in a prayer meeting yesterday. We all prayed for you and I was sorry for you so we wrote you letters. I'm 9. We're very thankful that you are coming out of hospital soon.

With love from
Sarah Newberry

Dear Owen,
I heard about your accident. Hope you're out of hospital soon. We've prayed for you. I'm seven years old, eight in July. I go to a Christian school and I read the Bible every day. I have one brother and one sister. With my mum and dad, we're a Christian family.

Love from Benjamin Palmer, 8
The Cedars School

Dear Owen,
I would like to give you a verse from Ezekiel 37 v 7: 'So I prophesied as I had been told. While I was speaking I heard a rattling noise and the bones began to join

together.' I thought that would go together with Jesus healing you.

Love,
    Shaun McDonnell, 7 years old

Owen m'dear,
A friend of mine has become a Christian recently – brilliant! His name's Stewart. Please could you pray that God will really nurture (kinda religious-sounding word, eh?) him and keep him safe from hassle from the enemy? Ta.

We had a mission on at the university recently, which hopefully will have got folks thinking. Mind you, some of my friends reckon it's all very well for us 'freaks' who're 'into religion', but that they don't need it, thank you. Maybe I could kidnap them and subject them to a Cliff Richard tape for a couple of weeks, denying them food, drink, fresh air and trips to the loo until they submit. . . .

    Your ole buddy,
        Cathy

Dear Cathy,
Thanks a lot for your copy of Psalm 46. It was very inspirational. Thank you also for your prayers. Keep them coming! I have just got on to the book of Job now in my reading. It seems as though he asked himself and God a lot of the same things that I have asked.

You asked me what my situation is like now and what I thought about it all. I know everything will be all right – that something good will happen, and that it is just a matter of time. Hopefully sooner rather than later. Over the last couple of weeks there have been a number of improvements: in my breathing, for example. The amount of air I have been blowing out has increased dramatically. The feeling in my arms is a bit better and the mobility in my neck and shoulders has also improved.

Of course the first nine months were the most difficult, psychologically and physiologically. But that's over now and I will just say that there is no doubt in my mind that eventually it will as you say all be used for the glory of God. This can't be bad!

What would you have said if six months before my accident I had come in one Sunday announcing that I had visited a church service? I think you would have been surprised, would you not? I believe your reactions will be a little different when I say I was at the Prescott Fellowship on Sunday and I really enjoyed it. I'll be going again! It would be even better if you could come as well, eh?

Cheers and God bless,
Owen

Dear Owen,

I read something in Michael Wilcock's Bible Commentary lately that I thought might interest you. It's from the chapter about 'The Purpose of Tribulation in the Christian Life': '. . . the Church is not a company of people who enjoy a trouble-free life. Neither, on the other hand, should it be a community inundated with troubles and no more ability than anyone else to cope with them. The miracle which the Church should both embody and proclaim is the POWER to cope with the evils of life.'

Have you ever thought of doing any counselling, say, at the Billy Graham Livelink Mission? You might shrink away at the very thought, but maybe you could really help some folks who're curious/confused about Christianity. . . .

See ya,
Cathy

Dear Owen,
'Hear the voice of my supplications, when I cry unto
thee, when I lift up my hands towards thy holy oracle'
(Psalm 28). 'Give unto the Lord, O ye mighty, give unto
the Lord glory and strength' (Psalm 29). Hope you feel
better soon!
    Love from Lucy-Emma Bones, age 7
        The Cedars School

Owen began writing a sermon for the preacher father
of another patient. Mark Harding, a Biology teacher
from Blackpool, was rock-climbing in Borrowdale
when he fell. But he was one of the lucky ones: he
suffered no neurological damage, and after eight
weeks in traction would walk again. Meanwhile, his
father visited him and met Owen. They discussed
their faith together and Owen agreed to write him a
sermon.

   Carol's small nephew was a bright lad who couldn't
have enough stories read to him. So Owen decided to
write one himself about Rodney the Red Tractor.
He was not, he assured friends later, imitating the
Duchess of York's helicopter stories. He could only
suppose, he said, that she had picked up on *his* idea.

Sybil phoned the BJA to find out what was happening
with Owen's insurance settlement. The cheque finally
arrived – seventeen months after the accident – and
was for £2,000. And despite Owen's appalling injuries
on that BJA-sponsored event, the association had still
not given any guidance to the individual clubs and
the many boys and young men in their care about
insurance coverage.

However, as a direct result of Owen's accident, individual coaches like Don Werner at Bracknell and George Edwards at Wigan put into effect new insurance policies for every lad in their clubs for £250,000 in case of similar injury.

Further gifts were sent to Owen and finally the Trust Fund achieved a total of £19,000. It meant that the Lowerys were able to purchase a specially fitted van for over £12,000. The remainder of the fund was borrowed, with Owen's consent, for a further deposit on the bungalow in Billinge, whose foundations were about to be laid in mid-March.

Chapter 20

'People have been sent to Owen just at the time he's needed it most,' Sybil said over a pub lunch with a friend. 'No one organises a thing, and yet there's always someone to laugh with him or pray with him. God knows just what he needs and when he needs it.'

Sybil was discovering that this applied to her too. A fair-haired, small, quietly spoken woman, she had found that her faith had not been broken by Owen's accident and the many complications that resulted from it. In those first days she prayed that his life would be spared. And it was. Then she prayed that he would be given something back. And slowly there were improvements in his movement and breathing. Then she prayed: 'Use him . . .' and she saw that happen in ways she hadn't dared imagine.

She had discovered her faith in her teen years, on her own. Perhaps because she had to reason it out for herself, because she hadn't been spoon-fed answers at an early age, her faith was all the deeper. But she was a quiet girl, not given to expansive conversations about her innermost feelings. She chose confirmation at the age of fifteen because it was important to her, even though perhaps others there were just coaxed and prodded by eager parents to 'do the right thing'.

Because the decision was a personal one, it never wavered. She didn't go through a period of disillusionment when spiritual idols fell. She never had them to begin with. It was always a very personal conviction between God and her. She simply believed him.

She was seventeen when she met Dave at a party in Reading. They were married four years later in 1968. He was from a Catholic home in Liverpool, and his widowed mother was very devout. But he saw only the negative, rigid aspects of his mother's convictions, and they made him sour about religion. Sybil was one of those rare people who could hold firm views and at the same time bear not one iota of resentment if others did not. She accepted Dave's lack of convictions and was never tempted to manoeuvre him to her ways.

When the boys were growing up, she believed that faith might grow for them in the kind of soil where her own had flourished. She didn't want them to feel pressured as Dave had been. It was her philosophy for their lives in general. She and Dave gave them every encouragement, every opportunity, but neither believed in leaning on them with their own opinions. When Owen's 'A' level results required a change of plan, she quietly accepted this and immediately went about finding alternatives. Even then she didn't press him with suggestions. She offered options and then calmly, cheerfully withdrew.

Perhaps her life was a preparation for these critical years. When friends asked, she insisted that nothing had prepared her to cope. 'It was just there to deal with,' she said, and anyway, she was just too busy to fret over what might have been.

Sybil found renewed spiritual strength from Owen's new Christian friends. She joined in the prayers, read some of the inspirational books they gave him and watched Christian videos passed on to the family. She attended meetings – sometimes just to act as chauffeur – and was blessed by them.

She was continually amazed at God's timing. Friends providing pastoral care for Owen seemed to arrive on a heavenly-arranged rota. Gordon Dacre was another one. He came suddenly and stayed briefly, yet his ministry changed Owen's life. On leaving to return home to Africa, he said, 'I won't be able to come back, but God will be sending you an angel soon.' And within a fortnight, Carol had begun to visit Owen regularly.

On June 12, 1989 the *Liverpool Echo* carried a front-page story and photo entitled: 'Crippled Judo Champ Falls For Nurse Carol.' The reporter thought she saw a 'scoop' during a Judo Training Weekend that Owen and Carol attended. She observed them together, asked a few questions and then had a photographer snap their picture. The couple didn't suspect her motives or the slant she planned for her feature. They were shocked when the article came out. The brief account contained many inaccuracies and misquotes. Above all, they had not wanted their private relationship to be paraded between the latest health warnings and lager lout incidents.

This relationship, as the reporter had observed, *was* getting decidedly romantic, but they were irked that a casual conversation could be used to announce a friendship they wanted to keep to themselves for the time being.

For almost two years Owen functioned as part of the hospital routine and machinery. He could not take a drink, turn a page, clean himself, switch on the TV or even roll over in bed without a nurse or attendant coming to his aid. Often he'd be compelled to wait for that sip of water or turned page because staff were involved in their own routine. Owen always understood this. He was aware that in hospital, as in the theatre, 'the show must go on' regardless of individual crises. Other more cynical long-term residents felt that patients' needs were a low priority: that hospital routine resembled an antique steam engine clattering and sputtering for its own sake.

Often a visitor would arrive at the Intensive Care Ward to find Owen still in bed at 1 pm or later, having been served no breakfast or lunch and not yet placed in his chair. Frequently the friend decried such neglect.

'Look, I'm not the only patient here,' Owen argued more than once. 'A new one came in this morning. They've got others to see to, and they're short staffed at the moment.' Only the most persistent visitor could get a single complaint out of him.

Even so it was obvious that since the accident Owen had lost not only his mobility and his independence, but above all his privacy. And despite his public achievements in sport, his gregarious ways with his friends and his constant clowning, he was a private person who was often reluctant to share deep thoughts with even his closest friends, and loathe to reveal his emotions even when others did so. Perhaps joking was one way of keeping his emotional life well hidden.

His fundamental need of privacy hadn't changed during his two-year hospital stay. His body may have become just another part of the hospital machinery, for any available nurse to service at her convenience, but the 'essential Owen' – his mind and spirit – was still very much his to keep as private as he wished.

Thus his deepest human relationship, his growing friendship, affection and love for Carol, was something he wanted to keep to himself. It hurt both of them to see it exposed to the public gaze like a piece of hospital laundry slung over a line.

They were the same sort of people, really. Even though Owen was joking and lively he was quiet underneath, deep and thoughtful. She realised that from her second or third visit to his room. And perhaps he knew then, too, that she was a bit like that as well.

They found they could talk about all sorts of things together. Carol had one or two close friends, like Alison with whom she played badminton, but she never was the sort to go around with crowds of people. She always did prefer a single friend. Even then she took her time getting to know the person and sharing confidences.

It wasn't just that he was easy to talk to. He had something – a kind of extra dynamic – that one doesn't see everyday. Some of his friends had it, too, like John Patterson who came often.

Owen said that it was because John was a committed Christian. They began to talk about religion and faith, and Carol said that she'd almost 'gone forward' at a Billy Graham Crusade at Anfield Stadium in 1984.

'Why didn't you?' he asked her.

'I don't know,' she said. 'I felt I should, but then I just didn't go. Something seemed to be holding me back.'

'It's normal to feel that way. It's something we've got to get past. We can't let anything hold us back from getting something more out of life.'

Carol agreed, and said she'd be willing to go with Owen to one of John's college meetings. It sounded interesting: they were organised for Catholic and Protestant students in Liverpool, and a black gospel choir would be singing.

One evening, at Owen's request, John Patterson came along to speak with Carol. It seemed to Owen that she wanted to take the step, but he felt he needed John's way with words to help her.

John was, as always, full of energy, buzzing with enthusiasm for telling people about Jesus. Owen remembered how his own excess energy had been channelled into judo, but although John too was a keen judo sportsman, that wasn't where his greatest energy and devotion lay. For him, the real challenge was in following Christ.

'It takes people with bottle to follow the Lord,' he said then, refuting the popular impression that religion is for cissies. He spoke of commitment as something that's best done when one is young and ready to take up life's challenges. 'God deserves the best,' he said, 'not just the bones of our lives.'

Carol remembered the night at Anfield Stadium, when Billy Graham had urged young men and women to follow Christ. He had appealed to them to come forward and publicly declare their intention to commit their lives to him. She saw that by doing nothing that evening she had said 'no' to God. This evening she said 'yes'.

On the surface he looked OK. If anyone passed him during the day and asked, 'How are things with you, Owen?' he'd say, 'Not too bad, thanks,' and give a friendly smile.

In truth, however, it was not a good day. He was very cold (his body temperature was even lower than usual), hungry (he'd missed lunch), bored, annoyed and miserable. His neck was stiff. He had been roused at 4.30 am and he hadn't slept since, so he was tired as well.

He sat in his chair next to the bed, waiting for Carol to return. It was 6 pm and she had gone out to get some food around the corner. Now he was as much waiting for her company as for the meal he needed.

On her return she sat on the edge of the bed and opened up her turkey sandwiches and his salad and chips. She fed him the chips first while they were warm. He was so hungry she kept offering more chips, and then the salad, and he eagerly took each mouthful. His container was empty before she'd taken a bite of her own meal.

'My neck's a bit stiff today,' he told her at last.

'I'll give it a rub when I've finished this, OK?' she said, nibbling on her sandwich.

They usually had a lot to say to each other. They were forever with their heads together, whispering. Often Owen playfully dug into her shoulder with his own, rocking back and forth, nudging her lovingly. She was usually deep in conversation, or listening intently, those long-lashed, blue-grey eyes fixed on his face.

Today they were quiet. He was too out of sorts to talk, and she sensed his discomfort. She knew he preferred quiet when he was like this. It wasn't that he even told her. It was just something she sensed.

Carol got up from the bed. She stuffed the wrappers and cartons into the paper bag and took them out into the hall and tossed them in the plastic-lined bin. 'OK, let's see what we can do with that neck,' she said as she returned to Owen's chair.

Her fingers were warm as they touched the aching spots. Gently she kneaded the flesh around the back of his neck, behind his ears, and then moved her fingers down the sides of his throat, rubbing his shoulders. She was talking softly to him, but for those moments he had suddenly slipped away, out of the room, out of the hospital.

The strange thing was that wherever it was that he found himself, Carol was there too, suspended in a cocoon with him. But the first thing he noticed was not himself or even Carol. It was the whiteness, the purity! And then he sensed that he and she – but no, it wasn't 'he and she', it was the eternal essence of each of them, the bit that is real – merged and blended with that whiteness. As it was happening, it seemed like forever. There was no 'he and she' – there was just the oneness blending in the light.

The next moment he was back again in the hospital room, in the wheelchair, in the confines of his body. And he wasn't sad to be back. He was exhilarated and the heaviness of the day was gone. It was not the first time that at his lowest point God had invaded his physical dilemma and shown him a glimpse of the eternal world ahead.

One afternoon Carol told Owen that she had discovered something in her Bible reading. She pulled a Bible from her kit-bag, and opened it where she'd kept a marker. She sat down next to his chair and put the open Bible on his knees. They read together from John 9:

> As he went along, he saw a man blind from birth. His disciples asked him, 'Rabbi, who sinned, this man or his parents, that he was born blind?'
>   'Neither this man nor his parents sinned,' said Jesus, 'but this happened so that the work of God might be displayed in his life. As long as it is day, we must do the work of him who sent me . . .'

'As I was reading this,' she said to him, 'I felt God saying that the work of God would be displayed in your life. It wasn't your fault the accident happened, you weren't being punished, but God is going to use you somehow for good.'

Sometime later a friend wrote to Owen and asked him why God allowed suffering. He remembered that passage and 'typed' it out on his computer. Then he added:

> God cares about all our sufferings far more than we ever imagine. What we must remember is that suffering is only a temporary state for all Christians.

It will eventually be eased either in this life or the life eternal.

Through suffering, God's love can occasionally shine more brightly than would otherwise be possible. For example, if someone afflicted in some manner can appreciate God's love then it can make non-Christians stand back and say to themselves, 'Why am I incapable of doing so?'

Suffering could also be God's way of reminding us that life on earth is not meant to be paradisiacal. If it were, how could heaven be better?

Owen's computer proved as much of a lifeline to him as was his ventilator. Then six months after he had received the long-awaited computer, it was taken away from his bedside and locked in another room on another floor, available only if staff were free to get it out. There had been a sudden change in the room arrangements and Owen was taken out of his ward and placed in a narrower corner of another ward which left no room for his computer or the many cards, pictures, photos and posters that had given some semblance of home to his bedside for almost two years.

Sybil approached the consultant to ask for his help. 'The computer doesn't belong to Owen anyway,' he said. 'It belongs to the hospital and it has only been lent to Owen.' He said that although Owen would be permitted to use it for as long as necessary, it was not his property so he would never be able to 'trade it in' or upgrade it for a more advanced model at a later date.

Amazed, she contacted BIT 32, the Liverpool firm

who had supplied it. 'It was bought by the hospital,' their spokesman said. 'We are not interested in who owns it.'

Sybil wrote to Martin Duffy of Granada, who assured her that it was bought for Owen and that it belonged to Owen.

Nevertheless the computer remained locked up on another floor and Owen lost that little bit of independence he'd enjoyed for six months. He, Carol or Sybil sometimes asked nurses to let him use it, but they were usually too busy and after a few times of waiting hours to be taken to it, Owen gave up, reasoning that he'd be home in a few months. Hopefully he'd be permitted to take it home if the matter was sorted out by then.

Chapter 21

Mark Sutcliffe was another young student assigned to Southport Promenade on a college placement programme. He was studying occupational therapy at St Catherine's College, Liverpool.

Mark met up with John Patterson in the college dining room and over their lunch trays they discovered that each of them had been leading a small prayer group to pray for their college. Muscular, effervescent sportsman John, and Mark, a quietly-spoken, slimly-built and studious-looking occupational therapy student, looked an unlikely pair to join forces, but that day they knew God had given them a job in common.

St Catherine's, a Church of England college, had recently been amalgamated with the College of Christ and Notre Dame, so the total student body was a mixture of Protestants and Catholics. In this ecumenical setting Mark and John had, independently, wanted to arrange meetings where students – whatever their family persuasion – could hear about the living Jesus Christ today, and what he wanted to do for their lives.

The two Christian students decided to work together to plan special meetings. John also told Mark about a young lad he had visited, named Owen. Mark told him, 'I've already been praying for him.'

Prayer to both Mark and John was a serious business. It was not just a question of casting one's mind over a list of family and friends at bedtime, and asking God – whoever he is – to bless them. Prayer to them was essential to their spiritual training programme and part of their daily spiritual exercises. It also included sessions with like-minded friends, who brought their own requests and needs for all to share. And it meant watching for, and expecting, God to answer them one by one!

Now Mark was looking forward to his placement at Southport. He expected to gain good experience, and he looked forward to seeing Owen again. They had met at several meetings and Mark sensed there was something special about the young patient.

Since Mark was assigned to occupational therapy rooms not far from Owen's Intensive Care Ward, he could pop over on his breaks or at lunch times. Invariably he'd feed Owen as well as himself, and staff were so used to seeing him there, they never knew whether he was in the room on business or for pleasure. Mark kept Owen supplied with books, tapes and videos to help him in his Christian life. His most valuable contributions however were probably the regular prayer times and teaching sessions that gave a deeper meaning to Owen's faith.

One day Mark shared something he had discovered about man's 'genotype' as opposed to his 'phenotype'. He had learned in his studies that the genotype was

the blueprint for one's body growth: the unseen potential which determined that one's hair/eyes/build were
going to be such-and-such. Man's phenotype, Mark
said, was that which could be seen: what actually
happened.

'The same thing exists in the spiritual,' he said.
'God has a genotype, a plan or blueprint for you. He
knows what you're made of because he formed you,
and he knows what you're capable of being.

'But the spiritual phenotype does not always match
the genotype. We often fall short because of our own
spiritual laziness, or because we allow Satan to thwart
God's plans.

'It's important that we always come to God and
say, "Lord, what would *you* have me to be?"'

Brian, Owen's first 'personal chaplain', had been
ordained and inducted as pastor of Bethel Mission, St
Helen's, earlier in the year. His ministerial duties
were now in addition to his full-time teaching post in
Rainford. Brian found himself with less time each
week to do all that needed to be done.

He wasn't the sort to say, 'I just can't do any more.'
He always saw some other need around the corner,
some other soul to help. But his schedule became
overloaded and it saddened him that he wasn't
visiting Owen as much.

He needn't have worried. With Mark on the spot,
there was always someone available to chat or counsel
whenever Owen wanted. Mark's sensitivity to people
and his spiritual discernment was another link in the
chain of people 'being sent to Owen' as Sybil put
it.

Cathy came unexpectedly one day and found a very grumpy Owen sitting in his chair. 'Hey, champ, this isn't like you,' she teased him.

'Try dealing with some of these characters and see how you like it,' he muttered.

It was one of those days when he wondered what God was doing with him. He hadn't managed his breathing time very well and was discouraged. Then Mark came in and urged him to 'praise the Lord anyway' which did not have the desired effect. Mark, usually capable of lifting his spirits, had failed this time.

'I didn't want to take it out on the nurse,' Owen said, 'but it wasn't the best time for her to say she was too busy to get the phone for me.'

'That sounds ominous,' Cathy laughed, and it made Owen grin.

They talked about 'what God was doing with him', and Cathy said, 'Just think, before you believed in him you had no one to blame!'

They prayed together then and by the end of the visit Owen was back to his old self and had completely forgotten his earlier frustrations. They looked over at Tom Bernard, a four-year-old black boy from Sheffield, who'd been brought in recently. Having been struck by a car, he was, like Owen, a tetraplegic and on a ventilator. Now he sat in his wheelchair, alone, watching a video.

Suddenly Owen felt grateful. 'Tom's never had a chance in life,' he said to Cathy. 'I was given years to develop my sport, to travel abroad, to experience many things. I've had my life! But what about him? He won't be able to enjoy any of that.'

A young sandy-haired Irishman passed by Owen's bed on the way to visit his recently-injured wife, Julie. Her bed was at the opposite end of the Intensive Care Ward. He cheerily greeted one of Owen's visitors and they started up a conversation. A building worker living in Rochdale, he had two small children to look after now, despite his labouring job.

'How are you coping with everything?' he was asked.

'OK,' he said, calmly, cheerfully. 'The people at church have been so helpful. . . .'

Gradually the story emerged of a young alcoholic suffering from ulcers, who the year before had agreed to attend a meeting in his wife's Baptist church. Raised in a Catholic section of Belfast, Maurice had a few preconceptions to overcome, but he was welcomed warmly, and even prayed with for his physical problems.

Two things happened to him that night: he was healed of his drinking problem and he became a born-again Christian.

'How did your family back home like that?' he was asked.

'At first, not very well,' he smiled. 'But recently my mother went to a healing meeting herself and let them pray with her! She sees a change in me, and that's surely to the good.'

As Maurice rejoined his wife, the theme from *Neighbours* rang out from a nearby telly. 'Not that again,' Owen moaned. He hated that bunch on Ramsey Street. 'John!' he called out, 'how about putting on my earphones?'

For a decade, the Norbreck Castle Hotel, on Blackpool's North Shore, has been the venue for lively
conventions of the British chapters of the Full Gospel
Businessmen's Fellowship. The robust spirit within
the FGBMFI makes it a place where the men expect
great things to happen. In August 1989 members and
their families again travelled to the hotel for five days
of teaching and fellowship.

Owen, Sybil, Carol and Mark arranged to travel in
the hospital van to the Friday dinner meeting. Carol
and Sybil walked briskly ahead of the wheelchair,
finding ramps, making sure doors were wide enough.
In the airport-hanger-size auditorium they searched
for sockets near a table in order to hook up the
ventilator. When Owen travelled, the portable ventilator carried on the back of his wheelchair was a
convertible type, which ran off batteries outdoors or in
a van, but used mains electricity wherever possible for
longer periods.

Inside the auditorium, well-placed sockets were
found several yards from an empty table. Carol pulled
a roll of tape out of her kit-bag and swiftly taped the
extension cord to the floor, as it was a thoroughfare
used by waiters carrying trays of food. The party was
seated with a minimum of fuss, and Carol and Sybil
took turns feeding Owen the roast beef dinner.

During the meeting that followed, Owen was called
to the front for special prayer. Don Latham, principal
officer of Bath County Council, led this period and
ministered powerfully to Owen, praying with the
laying on of hands. More than 500 others focused their
prayers and love on him, which was also keenly felt by
Carol, Sybil and Mark.

A physiotherapist came forward to join in the circle around Owen, and as the praying continued, she reached down and felt his diaphragm twinge – although according to medical opinion this no longer functioned. Owen felt a sudden surge of strength and moved further forward in his chair than he had done previously. And later, when there was lively singing and dancing to the Lord throughout the hall, Owen's upper body beat against the back of his chair, 'clapping' with every muscle available to him.

Weeks later he was asked, 'What were the results? If a person is still in a wheelchair, how can it have helped?'

'It's difficult to put into words,' Owen explained, 'when it's something of a spiritual nature. I know I've experienced improvement: in my breathing, in some of the feeling in my arms. But it was such an inspiration; so uplifting. I really felt the power coming through.'

Mark later gave him an unofficial sensations test, checking his feeling in both arms while he did not look. It was clear there was some new feeling in both arms almost to the elbow. There was no doubt in Owen's mind, or in the minds of his family and friends who looked on, that whenever people prayed there was a step forward.

Chapter 22

When he was competing, Owen's daily schedule of exercises and training had been essential. Now that he was paralysed, a regular regimen of exercise was even more important to his well being.

In the very early days at Southport, lying there without moving for many weeks had caused a lot of fluid to gather in his chest and this needed shifting. Owen couldn't cough it up on his own, so physiotherapists Felicity and Angela worked carefully to push on his chest regularly to invoke the necessary discharge of phlegm.

Later, as he was able to sit up, this was no longer necessary, but he followed a careful programme of exercises called 'passive movements' to maintain mobility in the joints and keep them from stiffening up. In the beginning, he lost movement in his shoulders and it was hoped that this could be coaxed back to life. His fingers curled up and staff or friends regularly opened up his fingers, gently stretching them to keep them supple. His neck was stiff and needed massaging. His knees, legs, ankles and heels had to be moved and exercised to keep them from locking and becoming unmanageable.

A visitor asked one of the staff, 'If a paralysed person can't use his limbs why must they be exercised?' The nurse patiently explained that the paralysed person must remain supple or how would it be possible to handle him normally, in bathing, turning or placing in a wheelchair? Furthermore, if he is allowed to stiffen up, there is the serious problem of bedsores or pressure sores. These can become infected and may even prove fatal. Finally, exercise is essential to reduce muscle spasms.

During the first months at Southport Owen was taken to the gym regularly. The physiotherapists worked hard to loosen his shoulder muscles and three times a week he endured the 'cage' to try to make progress.

Since a paraplegic or tetraplegic normally experiences most or all improvement in the first six months, physio staff devote their greatest effort during that time. But when they moved on to other newer patients, it was essential that Owen didn't give up. His friends thus continued 'training sessions' on their own. They put him through his paces, massaging his neck and shoulders, moving his arms and fingers and heels. On a few occasions the heels had been allowed to stiffen and Carol worked on them in thirty-minute sessions until suppleness returned. Regularly she lifted and stretched his arms as he sat in his chair, to retain mobility. When friends Lee and Shaun visited, they worked on his heels. John Donahue gave him shoulder massages with linament. Mark did neck massages when it felt stiff. And of course Sybil learned to do all these exercises, preparing herself for when he came home.

Pressure sores are always a threat to a paralysed patient. If he is examined carefully each day, turned regularly in the night and sits in a well-padded chair when he is up, he is usually able to avoid the dreaded sores. Even so, and despite skilled care, Owen developed several during his hospitalisation, and was then obliged to stay in bed until they had healed.

Owen's disability was greatly compounded by breathing difficulties when the implant operation didn't achieve the desired results and he was again obliged to depend on the ventilator. From the early months of 1988 he had experimented with his ventilator, asking the nurses to turn it off for short periods of time. It was like a workout: one day it might be ten minutes off the vent and then he'd gradually work up to twenty. Mornings were the best time to do his breathing training, before the nurses got him up for the day. Lying there in bed, he might be able to breathe on his own for half an hour or more, and on such days he'd feel encouraged by his progress.

Some mornings, inexplicably, he couldn't manage more than a few minutes. Then he'd be tempted to wallow in discouragement. He knew that wouldn't get him anywhere, however, so he'd call one of the nurses over to put on his headphones and he'd listen to a tape. And he'd tell himself that he could try again later in the day.

Owen gradually expanded his breathing time off the ventilator until he was able to breathe normally for several hours at a time by the end of 1988. The following year he achieved a personal best of seven hours' continuous breathing without the vent. This could only be accomplished though when he was reclining or almost reclining in bed. When he sat up in his chair, he found it far more difficult to breathe independently. At best, he could breathe without the ventilator for up to an hour when he sat upright.

Later Owen picked up a germ and had a chest infection. He had been given a flu jab to protect him against the influenza virus that attacked so many at that time, but he didn't escape another germ and this weakened his system. Afterwards, he wanted to resume his independent breathing, but knew he'd have to be careful after an illness. 'You have to take it fairly easy,' he explained. 'You have to stop before you tire; you mustn't let yourself get weak. If you've hurt your leg, you wouldn't go out for a long run, you'd have a gentle, fairly short one. You wouldn't want to wear yourself out.'

As Owen regained his strength, he gradually increased his times spent off the ventilator until he was able to breathe independently for almost two hours sitting in his chair.

Other procedures were necessary to assist Owen's breathing. He needed regular 'suck-outs' when phlegm clogged the tubes, and trachea tube changes to replace the discs and tubes for cleaning. These tasks were originally performed by staff, but in time Sybil, Carol and a few other friends learned how to help when necessary.

Elimination of body waste is another problem for the paralysed person. A female patient has a permanent catheter inserted into the urethra and urine flows into a 'leg-bag' concealed under dress or trousers. A male patient wears a condom-shaped fitting with tube outlet for the urine to flow into his leg-bag. The tetraplegic is unable to regulate his own bowel movements so a nurse inserts a suppository at a certain time every other day, and then removes the waste with a gloved hand. If the patient eats a well-balanced diet, this encourages a high degree of regularity. This procedure, compared to the use of enemas or laxatives, most clearly approximates a normal function.

An additional problem facing the tetraplegic is lack of body heat. The absence of movement limits circulation and the body can experience severe cold attacks. There were occasions when Owen was so cold that although he was sitting in a warm room he was dressed in several sweaters, a thermal jacket and three thermal blankets tucked from chin to toe. And still he was cold!

All these procedures were a necessary part of the daily care of each paralysed person at Southport. Visitors who walked through the archway marked 'Regional Spinal Injuries Unit' were often shocked to see how many young men filled the beds in those wards. But even these were only a fraction of the paraplegics or tetraplegics who must adjust to life first in hospital and then at home with family to care for them.

It is estimated by the Spinal Injuries Association that there are about 500 new cases of spinal injury each year. These are distributed throughout the twelve spinal injury units in Great Britain and Ireland. And although exact figures have not been collected as yet, the SIA calculates that there are between 20,000 and 30,000 sufferers in these islands.

Of this number, roughly half are paraplegics and half tetraplegics.

The 10–15,000 tetraplegics alive today (many in hospital, some in special facilities, others at home) probably would not have survived a generation ago. Modern respirators have given these severely damaged victims an extra chance of life, and portable respirators or ventilators allow them to be mobile and to travel.

The most severe injuries of all affect the brain as well, and it is further estimated by the SIA that 10% of spinal injury victims are also brain damaged. The Association for Head Injury victims believe that about 4,000 per year receive some sort of head or brain injury. In most of the spinal or head injuries, the victims are male, between eighteen and thirty. Sporting and auto accidents are the main cause.

At Southport, in the 'G' wards surrounding the Intensive Care Unit where Owen lived, dozens of other young men were recovering from their injuries, lying in bed or moving along the corridors in their wheelchairs. Some, unable to wheel themselves, were pushed to a sunny spot near a window to view the outdoors. A few sat together, wheelchairs facing, in the corridor. One young lad, his limp hands resting on a cushion, read a magazine, turning the pages by means of a rubber-tipped stick which he held in his mouth.

Chapter 23

Building on the 1,500 sq ft bungalow continued apace. It had earlier been forecast that it would be completed by July, but now that date was amended to the end of September. Workmen started on the walls in May and these were up the following month. The roof was on four weeks later. The electrical work, kitchen and bathroom supplies were next on the list.

Most weekends Sybil and Dave would drive through Billinge and round the curved Sefton Fold Drive, hoping when they turned the last corner that some progress had been made. The track was muddy and rocky, with mounds of soil piled everywhere. It seemed sometimes that there were as many months to the finish of it as there had been at the first. And with each month it was delayed Owen waited.

Dave had ideas about the back garden and he was anxious to begin work on it. He wanted to build a small pond outside Owen's window, but he planned to build it on a raised mound so that Owen could get a good view from his chair.

Dave and Lisa Riding from Preston were another couple who didn't miss a week. Shortly after the accident while attending a Christians in Sport dinner, a vicar from the Reading area came over to their table and asked them if they'd look in on a lad from Reading who'd been injured.

That was almost two years previously, and their Tuesday night visits were now an enjoyable part of all their lives. There were dinners in Southport and at the Ridings'. And they'd recently hosted the Lowerys and Carol at a Preston NorthEnd v Reading football game. One week they told Owen about a school reunion they planned to attend a few days later.

'Better keep your eyes open,' Owen warned Lisa. 'There might be some old girlfriends lurking about, trying to take him off your hands.'

They all laughed. The Ridings still acted like newly-weds after three years of marriage.

The following week Owen asked about the reunion. 'Great time,' Dave said.

'Too bad about Irene, though,' Lisa teased him, and then told Owen about a girl who had asked David for a dance, and seemed to be talking with him every time Lisa's back was turned.

'It was nothing,' Dave laughed. 'I told you I have no secrets.'

Some days later he had more explaining to do. A letter had arrived for David from Irene, saying she had loved being with him at the reunion and she suggested that they meet for lunch sometime. It was signed 'Love, Irene.'

It was a while before they discovered that the 'love letter' had been typed on Owen's computer.

One night the Ogdens joined Carol and Owen at the cinema across the Promenade. Unfortunately the only film available that night was a horror story called *The Blob*. Soon after their arrival, Owen and Derek were threatened with eviction as their guffaws were rather spoiling the intended atmosphere.

'It wer' the stupidest picture ever made,' Derek pronounced later, 'about a blob the size of Wigan. It wer' a good picture for a laugh, though.'

Towards the end, Derek wasn't laughing. Owen had stopped breathing and Derek, panicking as usual, fled. Carol casually wheeled him back up the aisle and into a corner of the lobby, where she coolly gave his congested tubes a 'suck-out'.

When calm was restored, Derek reappeared. 'Is he all right?' he asked, eyes wide. 'That's why I went,' he tried to explain. 'I knew he wer' in good hands wi' Carol.'

Dot was horrified the first time she heard Derek threaten to unplug Owen's respirator.

'He wer' goin' on about our Manchester City again!' Derek offered in his defence. 'The lad's just a johnny-come-lately about Liverpool. He only supports them when ther' up top.'

'When aren't they?' Owen teased. 'Not like that miserable team of yours!' And they were at it again.

They often played games of an evening like *Quizmasters*, or *A Question of Sport*. After a while, Derek refused to play the sport game because, he said, Owen had memorised all the answers.

One evening while playing *Quizmasters*, Derek was stumped by the question: What is a quadriplegic? He scratched his head. 'I know I've heard that word before. . . .'

Finally Owen laughed. 'That's me, fool! Fancy you coming here two years and not knowing that's me!'

Simon Lambourne popped in one day. He had been Owen's earliest sparring partner and they had scrapped at school as well as in the neighbourhood. Their first year teacher had labelled them 'the mafia', and soon after that their mothers had taken them off to their first judo lesson.

Simon, now a tall, strong-looking twenty-year-old, was working on a building site nearby. He brought Owen up-to-date with events in Reading, and told him the latest news of some of their friends there.

Adam was brushing Owen's teeth, but then stopped to join in the conversation.

'Come on, gizmo,' Owen said through the tooth-paste, 'scrub 'em properly!'

'I can't get at them; your ugly great lips are in the way,' his brother replied kindly.

'Well, I'd best be off,' Adam said at last. 'I've parked in a disabled spot, but I seem to have left my sticker at home.'

They laughed. 'Be sure to limp to your car,' suggested Simon.

'Or close your eyes and grope crying: "Where is it? Where is it?"' Owen said.

'. . . and knock over a few people on your way out,' Simon added for good measure.

Mark Sutcliffe had just arrived for a visit when Cathy came through the door. She had driven over from

Sheffield, and appeared, not in the infamous grandad coat, but in baggy trousers held up by old braces over a man's shirt. After Owen had introduced them, Mark asked, 'What made you two such great friends?'

'I like scruffy people with no dress sense!' Owen joked.

'And I love obnoxious people,' Cathy rejoined, laughing.

Later Carol arrived and another chair was added to the circle. They chatted about Adam's 'A' level results. Owen told Cathy that his brother would be going to Loughborough, but he'd wait a year.

'What's he planning to do in the meantime?' she asked.

'He wants to work – at whatever will pay the most money!' Owen grinned.

'He wants to help with the family move and all the expenses, and earn some money for Owen,' Carol told her.

'Well, well! I take back everything I've ever said about dear old Adam,' Cathy said.

Little Tom, hooked up to a miniature respirator and tucked into a miniature wheelchair, called across to the lively group. He had some noisy rock music on his radio, as usual, but that wasn't the same as having a real visitor. 'Can you come over?' he called to no one in particular.

One of the group got up and took a pad and pen. 'How about some more writing practice?' she asked, extending the pen. He happily opened his mouth.

Mark was talking to Cathy about the group U2. 'Have you heard them do "I still haven't found what I'm looking for"?'

'Yeah, I've heard it,' she said. 'But I was sort of disappointed. If they're Christians . . .'

'I don't think they're saying they haven't found God,' Mark said. 'I think they're saying they're looking for more Christians to show the kind of love and concern the world needs.'

'Oh, perhaps that's right,' Cathy conceded.

'Anyone else ready for lunch?' Carol asked. 'I'm taking our orders to the Windmill.'

Carol returned later with a box of sandwiches and burgers and began to feed Owen his lunch. Cathy told Mark about her recent trip to Spain and about a street meeting she had attended there where local ex-drug addicts sang and danced in the streets, praising God.

Owen was busy gazing at Carol and the two of them had their heads together, shutting out the rest of the world.

Before Cathy took her leave, Mark suggested they all pray together and he drew the curtain around them for privacy. First he prayed and then Cathy, for God to touch Owen and bring more healing on his body, and to bless each of them and help them in the lives he wanted them to live.

Chapter 24

The summer wore on, with Sybil and Dave making weekly visits to the building site that was supposed to be their home. Friends marvelled at their patience when every week's delay prolonged the homelessness of the Lowerys.

Dave had found employment as a shop fitter in Liverpool. After spending every weekend for almost two years in Billinge with George and Jean Edwards, he now moved in with them full time and stayed for another four months.

The Lowerys' Reading home, after months on the market, was sold at last. Then, in the final weeks, the deal fell through. Thus they began again, realising that time was running out; that when the bungalow was completed, a sizeable amount of money would be due at once. And they were well aware of the sluggish property market in Reading. Recently, many homeowners there had been forced into sales at well below valuation, or into bridging loans that presented an even greater loss. So in one sense, their unfinished bungalow was a mercy.

Owen remained calm about his extended hospital

stay. Visitors compared notes and they had never once heard him grumble. It was now two years since he'd arrived in Southport and many asked if he was impatient to leave.

'It'll come,' he'd say, taking it in his stride. Even when he was moved and his computer locked out of sight, calling a halt to his creative efforts, he remained cheerful and full of humour.

Bonds with Carol grew. She arrived at 3.30 pm daily to feed him his first food of the day. It wasn't that the nurses didn't bother, but from early on he had disdained hospital food whenever his mother was available to bring in meals from nearby pubs and restaurants. When Carol began daily visits, he preferred her to feed him, even declining food brought by other guests who appeared at lunchtime. Carol's house on New Scarisbrick Road was closer to the hospital than to Billinge, so that helped to keep Owen content in his situation.

Other problems remained however. Carol's job at a local nursing home became a struggle. Long hours, overlapping shifts, last minute alterations to her schedule and clashes with her college course-work created worry and frustration. In June she resigned to seek work elsewhere and was denied unemployment benefit, despite months of effort, application forms and interviews.

Earlier in the year they'd had frustrations with hospital policy. It had been decided that Carol could no longer take Owen for walks, even into nearby Lord Street or for a pub lunch, until she learned the complete trachea tube changing techniques. Owen's precious times of freedom were withdrawn without consultation. They felt they were being punished for small pleasures.

Carol quickly learned the techniques and began doing them under supervision. Finally after a dreary spell of being 'grounded' they were free to go out again.

Patients sometimes face such high-handedness in institutions when decisions are taken without consulting them. 'Sometimes you're made to feel an idiot,' Owen said later, 'as if you don't have the brains to think out your own solutions to problems. It's often said that people forget to speak directly to the disabled, or to draw them into discussions. But why do hospital staff show the same attitudes they discourage in others?'

One day Owen was particularly cold. A nurse arrived and flung the windows wide open. He mentioned his chill and asked for his temperature to be taken. Staff didn't regard it as important and so didn't bother to check it.

Many hours later, the ward sister came along and, noting Owen's discomfort, suggested they take his temperature. In a rare outburst, Owen said angrily, 'You can keep your thermometer now! Why couldn't it have been done when I requested it?'

The ward sister scolded him for this, reminding him that the nurse was experienced and he was not.

'Experience is no excuse for being inconsiderate,' Owen retorted.

The ward sister had the last word. 'You're getting too emotional now; you're obviously not capable of discussing this,' she said, and walked off.

Owen spoke of the problem with friends after he'd

calmed down a bit. 'Doctors and those in high-level authority give the impression that they can't be wrong,' he said: 'Sometimes they make you feel you're not intelligent enough to make decisions. The patient needs to feel that he has some independence left.'

Owen always stressed that the ordinary nurses were fantastic. 'They work long hours in crowded conditions and with poor pay. They do their very best, and I can't say enough about them,' he said.

Suddenly there was a spurt of activity on the Billinge site and the bungalow took on the appearance of a finished building. But it was not all good news. The Lowerys' Reading home remained unsold and the builder would be demanding his costs within days.

Hurried visits and calls to the building society produced a new crisis. A bridging loan was approved, but it would cost £1,500 per month which was more than Dave earned!

For some days Sybil and Dave discussed the possibility of giving up the bungalow. There was no immediate prospect of a buyer for their Reading house. They could be burdened with escalating debts for a year or more. Should they withdraw and begin again? Dave said, 'We're going to keep the bungalow, come what may.'

Then a building society official rang Sybil. 'Your monthly payment will be £350,' he began.

Sybil was shocked. 'You mean, in addition to the £1,500?' she wanted to know.

'No, just £350,' he said.

An amazed Sybil learned that the society had reconsidered the arrangements and decided to increase the mortgage and lower the monthly interest charges. Shortly after that a call came from Reading to say that a prospective buyer had made an offer on their house.

A visitor said to Owen, 'Well, I suppose your leaving this hospital will be the best thing that's happened to you in the past two years, eh?'

He disagreed. 'No. The best thing was becoming a Christian. The next best thing was meeting Carol. Going home, that'll be the third best thing.'

Chapter 25

One Friday in November, Owen left Southport to spend his first weekend at home. It turned out to be an emotion-charged weekend, ending with bitter words.

'My expectations weren't high,' Owen insisted later when talking about it with friends. 'I knew it would feel odd. Remember I was used to living at the hospital for over two years. That had become home. Billinge was totally unfamiliar to me. I'd only been taken to the bungalow twice before, when it was little more than a building site. I didn't expect it to be home sweet home overnight.'

Sybil and Dave had worked hard to get the house ready for his first homecoming. The carpets were laid, furniture arrived at the last minute and Owen's bed and equipment were squeezed into his corner room overlooking Billinge Hill. Dave hurried to fit bookshelves in the lounge and cupboards in the hall. A friend from Wigan helped Sybil hem and hang curtains and Adam drove back and forth to shops collecting light fittings and bathroom supplies. Outside, the muddy track which would someday be a road was

filled with building equipment, but there was nothing
they could do about that.

The first problem seemed to be the temperature.
They had pushed the thermostat into the 70s, knowing Owen would need to be warm enough. He was
used to the night-and-day heat of the Intensive Care
Ward and it wasn't long before he complained of
being cold in the bungalow. Dave headed for the
thermostat and pushed the lever higher, and Sybil
piled extra blankets on Owen and tucked them round
his wheelchair. It still wasn't warm enough, Owen
reminded them several times. Eventually the temperature was in the 80s and three out of four Lowerys
felt they were in the tropics.

Sybil had planned Owen's favourite food for his
first meal: scrambled eggs, fish fingers and spaghetti.
It was a combination not to everyone's liking, but she
knew he missed this sort of food in hospital and she
looked forward to serving it to him. They meant to
open a bottle of wine to add to the festivities. In the
end, the meal was something of a disappointment.
There was such rushing to and fro to get various pieces
of equipment to make Owen comfortable that the
meal was cold before everyone was able to sit down.
And then Owen wasn't as hungry as she'd hoped he'd
be, and they were all too harassed to remember the
wine.

Sybil had bought thermal flannelette sheets for
Owen's maximum comfort and warmth, and when it
was time for bed she folded back the covers.

'I can't have these,' Owen declared. 'The hospital
uses linen!'

Dismayed, Sybil tried to reason with him. 'Try

them this once. You might find they're just what you need.'

It took careful persuasion and after lengthy protests Owen agreed to try them. Sybil prepared him for bed and at last all the chores were done and she turned out the light, her hand on the doorknob.

'Leave the door open,' Owen called out. 'It's too dark and quiet in here.' Newcomers to hospital routine often complained about the noise and light which prevented sleep. But after two years of non-stop ventilator noise (one each for six patients) and other assorted sounds all night long, Owen was used to the light and clatter and was unnerved without it. It took him a long while to drift off.

Sybil came in, hours later, to turn him in the night. 'You don't do it like they do in the hospital,' he grumbled.

The morning routine began at 8.30 when Sybil arrived to turn him again. 'I know, I know,' she teased. 'I don't do it like they do in the hospital!'

Owen was apprehensive about the day nurses. What if they didn't come in time? How could he be sure they knew as much as the hospital ones? Could they cope with all his needs? Would he get along with them? His anxiety grew and when the nurse arrived just after 10.30 am and managed well with all his procedures, he found himself worrying about the other nurses who would come on other days.

Sybil hoped his appetite would improve. She knew he ate very little in hospital. The food was one of Owen's favourite complaints. Sybil was sure that once he was home and she could prepare the food he liked best he'd begin to eat again. It would help raise his body temperature too, and they might be able to lower the thermostat!

'What would you like to eat?' she asked him that noon.

'I'm not very hungry.'

'How about some soup?'

'No thanks.'

'Some cheese and biscuits?'

'Not yet.'

'When?'

'In a bit. . . .'

Sybil didn't realise this was to be the usual daily refrain when he came home for good. She made up her mind she wouldn't worry about it, but when the time came to get him to eat, she found her stomach churning all over again, like a new mother with an undernourished baby. She began to conclude that he never actually felt hungry. He ate mechanically when he could no longer avoid it.

Owen had worries of his own. How would Carol get over to Billinge regularly? His mother would have to fetch her in the van, but what if she wasn't available? Owen sat looking out of the large picture window in the lounge, watching the workmen carry piles of equipment to the unfinished cottages across the road. This spot seemed very remote, isolated from all he was used to. He thought of Carol's short bus ride to the hospital, the ease with which she pushed him across the Promenade to the cinema, or to a show at the Floral Hall. He remembered the warm evenings along the sea front, just steps away from the ward. Pubs and restaurants were round the corner.

Here he felt so cut off. He wasn't sure he wanted to

come home at all. In fact, this was just a house. Hospital was home.

In the afternoon, Dave drove to Southport to pick up Carol. As soon as she arrived, Owen asked her to wheel him into his room. They sat there together, talking quietly. Soon they found themselves whispering. It was an eerie, uncomfortable feeling: the hush of the house, the absence of people milling about. Owen asked Carol to play a tape, and the loud throbbing music cheered him up a bit and made him feel more relaxed.

'Do turn that down,' Sybil said from the doorway. 'It's very loud, Owen.'

'We just want to listen to some music!' he complained. No one ever objected at the hospital, he thought to himself, recalling six TVs or radios all blaring at once. Here the silence was getting more and more depressing.

Sybil had set up the computer next to his bed, ready for him to use. She knew he was anxious to get back to his correspondence. A pastor was waiting for him to finish a sermon he had started, and there were several essays promised to other friends that had been interrupted when the hospital staff had taken away the computer. Fortunately, that problem had been resolved, the hospital saying that Owen 'could have it on loan for an indefinite period'. Sybil thought that after months of inactivity he'd be glad to tackle his writing again. She thought he might enjoy a few hours on it this afternoon, and couldn't help remembering how long it had taken her to set it up and get the environmental controls right. She told herself that this was only the first day and tried not to get annoyed about it.

A succession of friends dropped in that evening and Owen entertained them all in the lounge, like a host at a houseparty. Later when he became tired Adam pushed the chair into Owen's room and other friends visited him there.

The following afternoon Dave took Owen back to the hospital, but not before Owen and Sybil had exploded at one another. He accused her of expecting too much from him; Sybil felt he wasn't even trying to appreciate their efforts.

'Well then I might as well go back to the hospital!' Owen stormed at his mother.

'Go back there and stay there, for all I care!' Sybil cried.

Dave frowned at them both and then, without a word, wheeled Owen out to the van and helped him inside. Sybil stood in the hallway, distressed and bitterly disappointed. 'I suppose,' she told a friend later, 'we were trying too hard.'

There was a truce the next day when Sybil arrived at the Intensive Care Ward. They grinned at each other, remembering their anger and frustration. 'It's going to take some adjustment, Owen, for both of us,' Sybil said.

Owen knew that his mother would have to adjust to a very different lifestyle when he got home. She had enjoyed her work at Reading University and had appreciated the social contacts there too. She spent few days on her own at home; at weekends she was off shopping and visiting her parents nearby. It would be a marked change to sit at home and 'babysit' for an indefinite period.

Owen realised that soon they would be alone

together more than at any other time since his child-hood. In Reading he had spent little time at home. He hadn't made a habit of studying at home and it was mostly a case of rushing in, changing clothes, running out again off to the judo club or playing tennis with mates. Sometimes, late for a match, he would grab a stand-up meal in the kitchen, unable to wait a few minutes and sit down with the others. Weeks would go by without him spending a night in with the family. Sybil's work schedule and his activities hadn't left much time for the two to sit and chat. All that would change.

Chapter 26

When Dave Lowery wheeled his son back into the Intensive Care Ward he got the impression that Owen was glad to be back. The weekend hadn't gone quite as they had expected, Dave thought to himself. No doubt they needed to give Owen more time to get used to the new environment. He could see pressures growing with the normally-placid Sybil and Owen who was usually pretty even-tempered.

Owen was grateful to be returned to the familiar corner and see the familiar faces. Little Tom called out to him at once hurling child-like insults. Owen replied in kind, enjoying the exchange. Somehow the noise and bright lights were much more to his liking. He was glad when he was in his own bed.

During the next few days Owen reflected on his relationship with his mother. Had they ever been close? He wasn't so sure. They had spent so little time together it was hard to tell. They'd had clashes before, of course, but for the most part she had remained broad-minded and tolerant of both boys, even when they had made a mess of the house after a party, or had had too much to drink. Sometimes, as after his 'A' levels, she just moved in quietly and sorted things out for him. Well, he didn't want her to think she could organise everything for him now.

Shortly before his birthday, Owen was released to begin his new life at home. Sybil arrived at the hospital in their new van. The side opened up and the chair was hoisted into position facing the front. When they got settled with all of his necessary equipment, clothes, blankets and paraphernalia of the past two years tucked in all around him they were off.

They turned the corner out of the car park and moved into the flow of traffic along the Promenade. There was a final glance at the hospital. A large 'For Sale' sign, recently erected near the front wall, announced: REDEVELOPMENT POTENTIAL.

In the hospital van the chair had to go in backwards, like an afterthought or a person out of step. Now he and Carol and his mum all faced forwards, together, as Southport slipped by on each side of the road. They drove past Funland, Happiland and Pleasureland then down a side street, a mini Las Vegas, with arcades called the Golden Nugget and Little Caesars. At the lights the van turned into the boulevard of Lord Street with tall, handsome buildings from a grander age and shops where he took his first outing two Christmases ago.

It all slipped past him, his life of the last two years, and he mentally prepared himself for what lay ahead. It was like a judo match again and the time had come to change gears, to get ready for the serious business of living and competing.

One friend had warned: 'You might think it's a silly thing for me to say, but you will miss hospital. Home will sometimes be lonely. Your mother won't have a team of nurses to help. And the outside world will often be unhelpful, even unfriendly.' He was beginning to understand that already.

Hospital life had been like an endless game of tennis, full of sociability and routine. It was easier to go along with it all, to join in with the corporate routine rather than to create one's own. He hated *Neighbours* and *Coronation Street* but when the opening tune rang out from every other corner of the ward why fight it? He had learned to absorb the assorted background sounds and not to resist them. Little Tom might play his tapes louder than necessary, but that was his share of the communal cacophony carrying them all along. The constantly crowded room was just another part of the entertainment.

Owen recalled the times he'd been frustrated and angry with hospital regulation. What purpose did that serve? For hospital life to be tolerable one played according to its rules. Some patients complained that a hospital was run not for the convenience of patients, but for staff. Owen didn't agree with that any more. Everything one needed was immediately available. A quick trip to Lord Street proved this. Shops, roads, footpaths, pubs and public buildings were designed for walkers, not wheelchairs. In hospital, the wheelchair was the norm. Life was bearable in hospital. Outside it was not always so.

The hospital performed another important function. He was surrounded by others afflicted equally badly or worse. (Didn't George Bernard Shaw say

life is made tolerable by looking at others' mis-
fortunes?)

The hospital had become a friend, Owen realised.
Visitors might shudder at the thought of his two-year
'confinement', but in fact it had made life worth living.

Well, there would be one or two compensations in
leaving Southport, Owen grinned to himself. No more
ministrations from Nurse GBH and her long sharp
fingernails! He dubbed her that when accusing her
of 'grievous bodily harm' after some indelicate
manoeuvres to his person. But Mark, ever the peace-
maker, urged him to think of GBH as 'God bless
her'.

They drove through the small village of Billinge,
turning sharply to the right up the hill that divided
clusters of new houses from surrounding farmland.
Rows of tidy houses faced out over the green countryside. What they lacked in garden space was well
repaid in the grassy views of sloping fields and an
occasional farmhouse.

The road curved and turned upwards through the
tight little community pressed on the edge of rural
Merseyside. Then it dipped down onto a newer,
unpaved cul-de-sac. Work was still in progress on a
converted barn and a few old stone cottages.

At the end of the cul-de-sac, on a little rise, stood the
new bungalow specially designed with ramp, wide
front door and entrance hall.

In the next weeks tempers flared, then subsided, then
rose again. Mark Sutcliffe arrived early one morning

while the nurse was doing her duties, only to be greeted with '*Get out!*' from Owen's room.

Sybil, looking more harried than usual, shrugged and walked into the kitchen and poured Mark a cup of coffee. She sat down at the table in the lounge opposite him.

'Who was the lucky recipient of that?' Mark asked. 'The nurse, you or me?'

'He didn't know who was at the door,' she grinned. 'He's very fed up at the moment. It didn't help that I couldn't pick Carol up this morning. He gets in a real state when I can't, but I have an appointment at noon. It takes longer than he realises. A few nights ago I took them to a meeting in Liverpool. It's not as easy as it sounds. I drove to Southport, back here to Billinge, then to Liverpool. I dropped them off then went back for them three hours later. Finally back to Southport and then at last home.'

'It will be good when she learns to drive,' Mark said. 'I'm only sorry I couldn't help that night.'

'Oh, it's not your fault. But Owen doesn't always realise all that's involved. He can only think that Carol must be here, come what may. Dave was working and Adam was at a match so it was up to me. Usually they help when they can.'

When the nurse had completed her chores and gone, Mark knocked timidly at Owen's door. 'Am I allowed in?' he asked.

'Sure,' Owen called, and when Mark entered he added sheepishly, 'Sorry about that. I didn't know it was you.'

'I'm glad it *was* me!' Mark said. 'Better for you to shout at me than someone else.'

Owen and Sybil, home at last

They spoke at length about Owen's frustrations and some worries that kept cropping up. Then they prayed together. That never failed to help.

'Are you ever tempted to blame God?' a friend asked Owen one day. 'Do you ever think, "God, what are you *doing* to me?"?'

'Sometimes,' he admitted. 'When I wind up with a pressure sore, I think, "Lord, what's the point of keeping me in bed like this?"'

'How do you pull yourself out of that mood?'

'Oh, Carol might come, and then I'd be OK. Or Mark, and we pray. Dad and Adam are good at getting my mind off things. They divert my attention, play games with me, talk about sport.'

Sybil was having lunch with a friend at the Waterside, a new restaurant on the East Lancs Road. She had the afternoon off since Lee O'Shaunessey had come to stay with Owen for his usual Wednesday afternoon visit. Lee was a great help because he had learned nursing procedures and could even do 'suck-outs' to Owen's trachea tube if needed. He also pitched in and helped reorganise Owen's jumbled collection of videos, tapes and books.

'It's such a relief to be able to come out like this,' Sybil said. 'It's very frustrating if I need a loaf of bread for lunch and no one's there to relieve me. I can't nip out to the shops even for ten minutes. It would be too great a risk.'

'I guess you're always glad when Dave and Adam come home from work.'

'Very often they arrive just in the nick of time,' Sybil laughed. 'If I've had a bad day with him Dave comes in and sizes up the situation. He doesn't say a word but just takes over and goes in and sits with Owen. Maybe I've struggled all day trying to get him to eat. One difficult day Dave came home and knew how upset I was. He went into the bedroom and as he talked, he casually took Owen's peanut jar from the shelf and started nibbling. Soon Owen said, "How about giving me a few?" And Dave in a relaxed way coaxed Owen's appetite to life again. In a few minutes he did what I had failed to do all afternoon.

'Adam's just like his dad. He'll come in and take over immediately. He might even say to Owen,

"You've upset your mum," but so quietly that it takes all the tension away.'

One of Owen's greatest frustrations was the feeling of being enclosed, of being unable to get into town in the chair. In Southport, Carol could push him on her own to pubs, shops or the seafront. Here, the NHS issue wheelchair was too heavy for her to push up the hill or over the rough terrain of the building site. And going downhill was almost as bad: she feared it could run away from her.

Even if they did manage the circuitous route through the housing estate there was only a small village shop and Post Office at the end of the journey. No Lord Street here.

Mark drove Carol over to Billinge one day and they visited Owen together. On the way home Carol asked, 'Do you think that if I accept him as he is it will block his healing?'

Mark replied that they each had to accept for the moment the situation in which they found themselves. 'Coming to terms with it,' he said, 'and trusting God for the future, is how to pave the way for God's will, not hinder it.'

A few days later Sybil spoke to them about this. 'I think some people have been unhelpful to Owen: those who came a few times, talked a great deal about healing and then disappeared. There was one pastor who came in clutching his Bible saying, "You've been in this bed too long!" He came for a fortnight and prayed fervently that Owen would be raised up. We haven't seen him since. I don't think that sort of caring is at all helpful. It's not the kind of thing God would do.'

'That's why I think Owen needs to become a part of the local Christian community,' a friend broke in. She knew he had not yet felt the need to join a local church. 'It would be a whole family of different people working together to encourage him regularly. Mark may not always be around. Right Mark? Aren't you finishing up your training in Southport soon?'

'That's right,' he said. 'I could get a new posting anywhere.'

'But if Owen becomes part of the local Christian community, there will always be someone on hand to help.'

Chapter 27

The first months were the most difficult. The feeling of claustrophobia continued. Long hours alone with his mother or waiting for Carol added to Owen's frustration. He couldn't get down to study or constructive work on his computer. Even the cheery room which he'd planned and thought about during the years at Southport seemed lonely and oppressive. As days passed he began to think there was a disturbing presence in the room. He felt uneasy and apprehensive. He shivered with cold and although Sybil kept raising the temperature he was still uncomfortable.

'Get Brian and John to come,' Owen eventually asked his mother. 'Ask them to bring Mark and Gary. We've got to do something about this place!' Sybil could see how anxious he was; did he think the room was haunted?

Sybil got through to Brian first. 'He needs you to pray with him,' she told the pastor on the phone. Brian said he'd come at once. Then she rang John. 'We'll be over this afternoon,' he promised.

Several hours later two motorcycles roared up outside the bungalow. Sybil opened the door to four leather-jacketed creatures with face helmets intact.

'My,' she smiled, 'you look like extras from *Blake's Seven*!' Then John and Mark, followed by Gary and Jill shed their gear and filed into the house behind her.

Brian had left an hour earlier after praying with Owen in his room. His other friends crowded round Owen's chair and listened as he discussed his unsettled feelings at home and in the room where he now lived.

It was a time to listen, his friends realised, not a time to give advice or to pass out platitudes. And even before they prayed together the atmosphere of love and genuine concern for their friend drove out all traces of fear and depression that had lingered in the room.

That day was the turning point for Owen; the house became home. Certain problems remained, but they didn't seem insurmountable any more. There would still be 'down' days, but somehow friends would appear at just the right moment to dispel the gloom. At last, Billinge was where he belonged.

When the editor of a judo magazine asked Owen to write about his new life in Billinge, he gave a tongue-in-cheek description of the village, to the amusement of some local residents and the indignation of others!

Chapter 28

The bungalow at the end of Sefton Fold Gardens was bulging with people on the night of Owen's twenty-first birthday. Seventy-two people piled in as friends from all over the UK came to celebrate with him. Many were in fancy dress. Sybil answered the door as Goldilocks, and Owen hid behind a magnificent bear outfit, until his ferocious head struck such terror into one young heart that it had to be put away.

John Patterson and his fiancée Alison appeared as Austrian dolls; David and Lisa Riding were 1920s 'flappers'. Carol came as Cinderella and Mark Sutcliffe arrived in a black-and-white striped convict suit, dragging a ball and chain.

A vast array of food was supplied by various women, and Carol's mum, Mrs Porter, provided a splendid cake in the shape of '21'. Balloons vied with people for house room and when Mark began setting off party poppers the avalanche of streamers threatened to bury all within.

Champagne flowed and those who didn't drink found themselves getting merry on the jellies. Before long it was necessary to issue a warning to drivers: avoid the highly potent jellies. Someone had substituted rum and vodka for water in the preparation.

There was plenty of music and a corner for dancing and all went well until Sybil burned the sausages. Derek came to her rescue and tried to cool them off with an impromptu juggling act. The still-sizzling sausages resulted in a livelier performance than poor Derek had intended.

In the crowded room strangers bumped into each other and introduced themselves. Invariably the conversation turned to Owen who linked them together. One marvelled at his calmness, another at his positive cheerfulness despite serious disability. An old friend explained, 'It's a family trait. They're all so placid; they seem to take life as it comes; they all have tremendous resilience. No doubt they're the only family that could survive such a situation.'

A newcomer suggested that Owen's new-found faith was the stabilising factor. 'He's looking beyond himself now. He knows this isn't the end. Besides, think of all the Christians who are praying for him. That's bound to have a strong effect too.'

A young woman had another view. 'It's not necessarily a healthy sign that he's counting on God to heal him sometime soon. It prevents him from dealing with his situation and confronting problems on a realistic basis.'

Her friend had misgivings about Owen's calm exterior. 'Don't you think it might be a cover-up? He doesn't seem willing to admit to depression or discouragement. That's not normal. Why would he want to disguise it? We're all human; we all get downcast. Are we to believe he never feels this way?'

'I don't agree with you. He doesn't pretend he's always cheerful. I've seen him become really angry. But I must admit he takes things better than I would.'

Another friend joined the circle and said, 'He must have some sort of outlet, some escape valve. What is it? Religion?'

'Maybe,' agreed another, 'but I think it's Carol. He shuts himself up with her and then nothing can touch them. It's as if no one else exists when she's around.'

'But she *has* been wonderful for him, hasn't she? She's so gentle and caring. You can tell how happy he is when she's with him.'

Speculation continued, but if the guests were expecting an announcement of any kind that night, they were disappointed. Owen fiercely guarded his relationship with Carol and she was equally mum about her feelings for him. Their special friendship was plain to see, but neither was willing to discuss it or where it might lead them.

One wag called the party a display of Owen's 'judo-Christian heritage'. Mark Sutcliffe found himself in conversation with one of Owen's new nurses. They compared notes on the occupational therapy profession and discussed staffing and facilities problems. Then she looked at Mark closely. 'Are you a born-again Christian?'

The question caught Mark by surprise. 'Well, yes, I am! Certainly! The problem is that many people don't know what it means. These days the term is used to describe all sorts of people who want a new start: like the actor who suddenly wants the world to know he's gay. Even a new car was given that label recently.'

'I used to think it was an American phrase.'

'Perhaps because there are so many American Christians,' he said, 'or because Billy Graham uses it. But it was Jesus, not Billy Graham or the Americans, who first said that we needed to be born again; that we needed to begin a new life in our spirits in order to enjoy a personal relationship with God.'

'I know Owen has that,' the nurse replied. 'I haven't known him all that long, but I can see that he has a real depth of commitment. I'm impressed with the way he doesn't hide his beliefs. And how he prays for people! But I can see that it has benefited his life.'

'Mine too,' Mark agreed. 'I certainly wouldn't go back on my decision.'

An old friend of Owen's from London noticed some Christian books lying on a table during the party. He went over to Sybil and asked her about them. 'They're Owen's,' she explained, 'but I read some of them too.'

'Do you?' he said with interest. 'I was given some Christian books myself lately and have been reading them. I must say they have started me thinking. And seeing Owen here tonight, well, he's got something I like. It would be good to come up and talk to him about it.'

'You'd be welcome anytime,' Sybil said.

Sybil told Owen about the conversation the next day. He was sorry they hadn't had a chance to chat. The crowd and all the noise had made serious talking difficult. But from that day, Owen began to pray for him.

Prayer was something that everyone could do. Owen saw the effects of it in his own life. Perhaps not quite as other people expected it. Maybe some expected a dramatic sudden change in his physical condition. Because that hadn't happened some might think prayer didn't work. Owen knew from personal experience that that was a wrong notion of prayer. He knew that when he prayed and when others prayed for him God never failed to give him new strength, both spiritually and physically. The last few times people had prayed for him at meetings and crusades he'd felt new strength and sensation, even in his hands. How could people explain that if they didn't believe God answered prayer?

He knew a number of people who had been helped through prayer in the last few months. Mark Sutcliffe's grandfather was one. He'd had a stroke and the prognosis was bad – until Mark and he had got together and prayed for the old man. Even as the words came out he somehow knew that something good was going to happen to Mark's grandad. And sure enough he made a remarkable recovery. Others could say what they wished about him being 'lucky'. Luck had nothing to do with it.

Then there was the nurse who asked for prayer for her daughter. The more he prayed the less he could fathom why so many people didn't tap into that source of power. God had answered too many times for him to call it coincidence.

Chapter 29

The Lowery financial problems continued. Their Reading house sale fell through again. Later one night Sybil and Dave reviewed the dismal situation. At the beginning of 1989 they had put the property on sale for £135,000. In March a couple offered £131,000 but backed out two months later when they couldn't get a mortgage. In July Dave had to drop the asking price to £120,000 as the slump had already begun.

With the Billinge bungalow nearing completion and the slump continuing, the Lowerys dropped their price in September to £110,000 or near offer. The following month they were relieved to find a buyer who offered £103,000. But in November their surveyor claimed that subsidence had been found and the offer was withdrawn.

Sybil and Dave were forced into a bridging loan which the building society lowered to £350 a month, but it only postponed the evil day: each month more than £1,000 was added to the total of the two mortgages.

In December the Lowerys paid almost £300 for their own survey of the Reading house to see whether the concrete foundations had indeed slipped. They knew that if the report was bad, they'd have to spend a vast sum on repairs. They also knew they couldn't pay yet another loan; the mortgage payments and bridging loan payment were by this time more than half of Dave's monthly income.

During the Christmas holidays the couple went over their sums again and again and reluctantly decided that the only way out of the mounting debts was to sell the bungalow and start again. They ruled out a return to Reading: Owen was determined to remain in the North with Carol and his other friends. Besides, Sybil's parents had moved to a nearby flat and had adjusted well to the upheaval. She wouldn't want to put them through that again.

The only solution was to move to a cheaper house, perhaps a small terraced one not too far away.

One Monday afternoon Dave's employer called him in to the front office. When he arrived home an hour later, he greeted Sybil with: 'I've just been made redundant.'

Never one to sit and fret Dave went out the next morning to look for work. By tea-time he returned home with a new job, as shop fitting supervisor with a Manchester firm. The only problem was that the hourly wage was less than he earned in Liverpool. But plenty of overtime was assured, to make up the loss.

Sybil had been grateful for Dave's help during evenings and weekends. It meant she could pop out to visit her parents once or twice a week and shop on Saturdays. However, that arrangement now came to an abrupt end. Dave was obliged to work seven days a week and he rarely got home before 8.30 pm.

'But what will you do?' one of Sybil's close friends asked her shortly afterwards. 'At this rate you'll never be able to shop or visit your parents or have an hour off. That's impossible!'

'One of Owen's nurses knows a local male nurse who might help out for an afternoon or two each week,' Sybil said. 'She's going to arrange for him to pop in soon, to meet Owen and see how they get along.'

'But who will pay him?' her friend persisted. 'Certainly your princely wage would be swallowed up in one afternoon payment!'

Sybil laughed. The government carer's allowance brought her £25 per week for her seven days and nights of 'attendance'. She fell back on a favoured phrase. 'Somehow it will work out,' she said.

In recent weeks a stuntman had been awarded over £250,000 in the High Court for injuries received while working on a film. He now walked with a slight limp and complained that he could no longer ride a horse. Leaving the court he said he was 'disappointed with the award because my career is over and I do not think the damages reflect that'.

When such items were brought to Owen's attention he didn't waste a moment brooding over them. Sybil recently described her son to friends as one with the ability to 'switch off' from thinking about unhelpful situations or making judgements about people.

'Just as it helped him in his sport, to cope with a setback and then return to the fray later on, he now doesn't bother to make pointless comparisons with others who may be better off than himself,' she said.

This attitude kept him from judging old friends who no longer kept in touch. One of his closest mates from school days stopped writing or visiting and didn't reply to letters inviting him up. A friend indignantly exclaimed, 'He's a dead loss, isn't he?'

'Don't say that,' Owen corrected her. 'Some feel more uncomfortable about it than others. It's not their fault that they can't deal with it.'

If one of his characteristics was the ability to 'switch off' and disengage when necessary, the opposite was also true. Owen was often stubborn, tenacious, obstinate and determined to hold on when he felt it was warranted. 'He's had to be obstinate to get as far as he did in judo,' Dave said in his defence one day. 'But I believe this tenacity also helps him now to keep bouncing back when problems come.'

If Owen's friends were curious to know what he thought of his permanent disability they hesitated to ask him. Some may have feared they'd be touching a very painful spot. Even his parents didn't press him on the subject. It took an ingenuous newcomer to confront him with questions others only thought about. And, as it turned out, Owen didn't mind at all.

'When did you realise you'd broken your neck?' Owen's inquisitive young friend asked him one day.

'I knew it at once; the moment it happened,' he said.

'Did you realise all it involved at that time?'

'No. I sensed that I'd broken it, but I somehow thought one didn't survive that. When I did survive, that gave me more hope.'

'When did the doctors tell you what you might expect?' he was asked.

'They never did tell me,' Owen said.

'But they told your parents!' the friend said in surprise. 'Why didn't they tell you?'

'Perhaps they didn't think I'd accept it,' Owen smiled. 'As it was, I had my own ideas. If they'd have given me a grim diagnosis, I wouldn't have taken what they said as gospel anyway. I still would've made my own mind up. I would probably have nodded as they said things and then carried on thinking what I wanted!'

'What sort of estimate did you set for yourself?'

'Oh, at first I hoped I'd be home for that first Christmas. When I came out of the hallucinations, I thought: I've got to come out of traction first. That will take six weeks.'

'They explained about that, then?'

'Oh yes; they put me in the picture about that.'

'And your trachea tube? Didn't they tell you when you'd be able to talk again?'

'Yes, they told me about that too. They explained that I'd have a changeover device fitted in six weeks, so at least I knew what was going on there. But they didn't tell me about anything else. They made no other forecasts or predictions to me personally. I had to guess on my own for anything else.'

'When did you revise those early estimates about going home?'

'By my birthday that November. I saw I wouldn't be ready by Christmas. And when they took me out that first time, to do some Christmas shopping, I knew I wasn't going to be ready for some time. I concluded that things might take longer than I'd thought to get better.'

'What did you think about the wheelchair?'

'At first I thought I'd be in it for a year or two. Or maybe three. But I never viewed it as permanent.'

'What about now?'

'I still don't. I never thought it wouldn't be all right – some day – but gradually I realised it was going to take longer.'

'When you became a Christian how did that affect your expectation?'

'I thought maybe it might not take so long to get better after all.'

'Do you still feel that way?'

'We-ll, I know God can and does heal. So anything is possible. But on the other hand, we can't predict God's timing, so it wouldn't do just to sit and wait for something to happen. You've got to get on with life as best you can, and do the things you can do.'

'Then, uh, how do you feel about things maybe being permanent?'

'I don't think this is permanent,' Owen said firmly. 'This situation is not permanent. If there's one thing I've learned this past year, it's that the spiritual world is going to be around a lot longer than the physical one. So it makes sense to get our spiritual lives sorted out most of all.'

'Do you mean you've given up the hope of having a physical healing?'

'Oh no. I'm just saying that it could happen in this life – or in the next. But this chair and this condition are not permanent!'

'He doesn't lose anything,' Sybil said to friends over lunch, 'by having this great hope, does he?'

One sceptic wasn't so sure. 'It could make it harder for him to learn to live in the here and now. . . .'

One of Mark Sutcliffe's friends asked him about this. 'Do you think Owen's accepted his disability?'

'I don't think I'd used the word *accepted*,' Mark said. 'I'd say he's coming to terms with it. He's learning to cope with life being paralysed. No one stops dreaming about walking, or having a small hope.'

'And you think he's doing all he can to come to terms with it today?'

'Yes, I do. Oh, perhaps I wish he'd study more, but then I wish I'd study more too! We could all do more to improve our minds and spirits, couldn't we? I'd say he has potential he hasn't used yet, but then that's good. We all need to work towards goals, to reach higher and achieve more. I think Owen will do this, but it will have to come from him.'

Chapter 30

Several of Owen's friends in various parts of the country couldn't stop thinking of the Lowerys' financial problems. Independently of each other these friends wanted to do something to publicise their plight and help ease the financial burden.

A new friend in Cheshire wrote to various newspapers, a charitable trust and even to Cliff Richard, suggesting a gala event for Owen's twenty-first birthday, to help him and his family. Only two newspaper editors replied and each discussed the possibility of a special campaign to raise funds for him. Hopes soared for several weeks. In the end, nothing came of the idea, apart from an article or two about Owen's accident.

George and Jean Edwards, the Lowerys' 'landlord' for two years, became increasingly more disturbed as mortgage and bridging loan problems grew. 'We ought to ask every judo player in the country to give a pound – just a pound – to help the family. That wouldn't be too much to ask, would it?' suggested George.

They discussed ways of approaching the 130,000 members throughout the UK. Perhaps each of the

1,200 clubs could be circulated, they said, if the local coach or secretary would contact each of his members. But then they realised that the postage alone would cost each club several hundred pounds, with more for the printing. From the beginning they had been involved in local fund raising, judo matches and raffles on Owen's behalf and were always urging friends to help too. Perhaps others wouldn't be so keen if they started yet another effort.

'But only a pound!' Jean exclaimed, getting used to the idea. 'That wouldn't hurt anyone.'

They continued to talk it over, but didn't seem to find any solution to the problem.

Pete and Gladys Knapp of Reading had known the Lowerys for fourteen years. Their own children were the same age as Owen and Adam and they'd travelled throughout the country from match to match just as the Lowerys had done. Pete's first recollection of Owen was of 'that bad-tempered little boy on a mat'. Then he watched him as he grew, winning more matches each year.

Pete found out about the Lowerys' mortgage problems too, and wondered how to help. A raffle? In order for it to have much success and wide appeal a large amount of cash would be needed up front for advertising, printing and gifts. How about if Owen were made a charity? He decided to have a word with a solicitor friend.

Just before Christmas, Jean and George Edwards travelled to Crystal Palace for the British Trials events. They found their seats and settled back to enjoy the day's activities.

A man approached, holding out some cards. 'Raffle

tickets, anyone? Buy some raffle tickets for muscular dystrophy!'

Jean looked at him and her mouth dropped. 'What?' she asked.

'Muscular dystrophy,' he said again. 'Want some raffle tickets?'

Jean exploded. 'Don't you know that charity begins at home? We've a lad who has broken his neck playing judo and his family is desperate for money! How can you forget one of our own who needs your help? I think it's disgusting!' she finished, almost in tears.

The man backed away after such a sound telling-off. Jean kept shaking her head. 'Something's got to be done,' she said to George, and he agreed.

When George bumped into Pete Knapp later in the day, they began to talk about Owen and the family. They discovered that they had similar thoughts about how to help. The 'pound-for-Owen' scheme came up again and this time they decided to go for it.

Meanwhile a teacher from Owen's old school in Reading read an article about Owen in the *Sunday Express* which mentioned a special wheelchair that would be a great improvement on the NHS one. The state-supplied model in Owen's words was 'built like a tank' and just about as difficult for Sybil or Carol to push up kerbs and steep ramps.

Owen had read about a Swedish model called the PERMOBIL that was much lighter in weight and could 'climb' up steps and kerbs, had a built-in ventilator, and computer-assisted steering that would allow Owen to manoeuvre his own chair by means of a 'sip and puff' device. The chair included front and rear lights, indicators, a hooter, word-processor and an infra-red beam control to answer the phone, draw curtains, open doors or operate the TV.

The PERMOBIL promised much greater mobility for Owen than other models, but the price remained the handicap: close to £15,000. Mr Springett, one of Owen's teachers at Maiden Erlegh School, felt that the pupils might raise the funds to provide Owen with his OWN PERMOBIL.

Chapter 31

Owen was busy typing out chapters from the Bible when some visitors arrived. With a barely perceptible movement of the head he positioned the cursor on one letter after another and with a faint puff on the curved straw the letter was added to his typed material.

'Why are you typing it all out?' he was asked. 'Isn't it just as easy to read from your easel?'

'Not when someone else must turn each page,' he replied, still blow-typing away.

'Isn't there a Bible on disk that you could insert into the computer?'

'Could be. I haven't found one yet. Anyway, it's not a waste typing it out. It's a good way to read and retain the verses at the same time. And once it's there it's so much easier looking up verses for reference.'

With another flick of the cursor Owen closed the computer file on John's Gospel and opened the next one on the Letter to the Philippians. In recent weeks he'd begun typing and studying Paul's 'prison epistles'. He was learning that while suffering the bonds of prison life Paul wrote the most extravagant statements of joy, praise, peace and contentment to be found in Scripture.

Owen was again a student after a two-year lapse. He enrolled for a London Bible College correspondence course in Scripture foundations. He was now busy with assignments but also recently completed blow-typing the whole of St John's gospel. In addition he was making plans to take a computer programming course at home with a St Helen's College lecturer.

'It's been quite exciting around here today,' Sybil said later that week as she greeted a friend at the door and walked him along the hall to Owen's room.

'What's happened?'

'We've been watching the Commonwealth Games and one of Owen's friends, Jane Morris, won a gold medal in judo.'

Owen told his visitor about his old colleague. 'We knew each other for years. Then Jane captained the Girls' Schools team when I was captain of the Boys' team. We travelled to judo meets in Israel and several European countries, playing for Britain.'

'Remember how you used to tease Jane by asking her how many brothers and sisters she had?' laughed Sybil as she brought cups of coffee into his room.

'She never could remember the amount,' Owen explained to his guest. 'Her parents fostered or adopted so many, the total varied each year.'

'Then, after Owen's accident, one of the first letters came from the Morris family – with a £100 cheque,' Sybil said. 'Imagine: with their family expenses! We were all overwhelmed.'

When Jane went to Auckland, Owen might have had bitter regrets that he was not there too, collecting medals himself. But he showed no trace of that; he was too busy rooting for Jane. When the visitor left, he got to work on his computer and designed a congratulatory poster for her. That Gold for Jane made his day.

'In the spiritual Olympics, Owen,' a friend told him later, 'you can still win a Gold. God has given you all you need to do that. It's up to you now to develop your spiritual muscle.'

Owen remembered the passage in Philippians that he'd typed earlier. It seemed to be written just for him:

> . . . one thing I do: forgetting those things which are behind, and reaching forth unto those things which are before, I press toward the mark for the prize of the high calling of God in Christ Jesus (Phil 3:13–14).

There was good news at last on the Reading home front. The surveyor engaged by the Lowerys thoroughly inspected the house on Falstaff Avenue and gave it a clean bill of health. He found no evidence of subsidence. It was one less worry for Dave and Sybil. For the third time in a year the house could go back on the market.

The two new funds discussed in the New Year were launched in February and organisers hoped to rally support and funds for these. Mr Springett of Reading launched his appeal for the much-needed PERMOBIL wheelchair at Owen's old school of Maiden Erlegh. Pete Knapp of Pinewood Judo Club in Wokingham and George Edwards of Wigan were trying to urge the

BJA to actively support the 'pound-for-Owen' fund, and encourage each member to do his part.

The male nurse appeared on the Lowery doorstep. He and Owen got on at once. Clive had been a hospital nurse who was himself injured and unable to work at a full-time job, but an afternoon or two a week suited him perfectly. Also he could do the 'suck-outs' and trachea tube changes that Owen needed.

His wage? 'Just a cup of tea will suit me fine,' he said to a grateful Sybil.

'What do you see for the future, Owen?' a friend asked one day.

Just as in the old days when he was training, he admitted that short-term goals were more clearly in focus than long-term ones. He was content for the moment with his busy social life, frequent dates with Carol, trips to concerts and crusades with some friends, and to shows and sporting events with others. And he was now enjoying being part of the Wigan Christian Fellowship of Billinge and developing new friendships there.

'My long-term plans,' Owen said at last, 'are in God's hands. I can't predict his timing.' Some nights later he spoke more fully about this at a meeting in St Mary's Church, Liverpool, his first public opportunity to acknowledge his Christian faith. The Revd Alan Godson, rugby sportsman turned vicar, asked Owen how Christ had helped him during the past two years.

'I know the situation is not permanent,' he said. 'I can't put a time limit on God, but in his time I know I'll be healed. It may not even be in this life, but it will certainly happen in the next. Meanwhile, I just keep faith, don't lose patience and get on with life.'

'Anyway,' Owen added, 'it's all for the glory of God, not man.'

> Lord keep me close, I care not how
> for I know thou wilt not allow
> one trial too many, one grief too much;
> for though to earthbound minds my life is dead,
> with thy sweet promises my soul is fed,
> until, please God, there comes thy healing
> touch.

Appendix

Current friends were not the only ones ready and willing to help Owen's 'redevelopment potential'. The SPINAL INJURIES ASSOCIATION, with headquarters in London, has branches throughout the country designed to help the disabled and their families, particularly as they leave hospital and seek to adjust to the world of the able-bodied. Many of those working for SIA are themselves disabled, either using the professional skills they acquired before their accidents or obtaining university qualifications afterwards. Baroness Masham, the president and founder of SIA, is an example of one who continues to lead a productive life. Other disabled SIA officers hold down demanding jobs at the London headquarters.

The SIA publishes books for the spinally injured, some of which are the stories and struggles of patients returning to life outside hospitals. The SIA also provides holiday accommodation for the disabled and their families in various countries, and a carer service for those who need a holiday from their twenty-four-hour-a-day schedule of care for the injured relative.

The fellowship of local groups helps to ease the post-hospital problems and adjustments.

> SPINAL INJURIES ASSOCIATION
> Yeoman's House
> St James' Lane
> London N10
> Tel: 01-444 2121

Mechanical aids are being improved continually. KEEP ABLE FOUNDATION provides a wide variety of mechanical aids from numerous countries to help the paralysed gain greater independence, including lightweight wheelchairs that can climb up kerbs and steps. Some wheelchairs are designed to house portable respirators, which benefit people like Owen. A variety of bedroom, kitchen and bathroom aids are available to make the patient's – and the carer's – life more pleasant.

> KEEP ABLE FOUNDATION
> 2 Capital Exchange Way
> Brentford
> Middlesex TW8 0EX
> Tel: 01-742 2181

In the United States, Joni Eareckson-Tada formed a ministry for the disabled called JONI AND FRIENDS INC. Joni was the young active sportswoman who became a tetraplegic and subsequently an accomplished Christian artist, singer, world traveller, writer and conference speaker.

Suggested reading:

Eareckson, Joni, *Joni* (Marshall Pickering, 1976).

Eareckson, Joni and Estes, Steve, *A Step Further* (Marshall Pickering, 1979).

Eareckson-Tada, Joni, *Choices . . . Changes* (Marshall Pickering, 1986).

Eareckson-Tada, Joni and Newman, Gene, *All God's Children* (Marshall Pickering, 1987).

Fallon, Bernadette, *So You're Paralysed* (SIA, 1987).

Fallon, Bernadette, *Able to Work* (SIA, 1979).

Maddox, Sam, *Spinal Network – the Total Resource for the Wheelchair Community* (Spinal Network, PO Box 4162, Boulder Colo 80306, USA).

Morris, Jennie (ed), *Able Lives* (The Women's Press, 34 Great Sutton Street, London ECIV ODX).